Long Ago in the Northern Palouse

An Anthology of Pioneer People, Places and Events

Compiled & Edited by Glenn Leitz

MARQUETTE BOOKS
Spokane, Washington

Copyright © 2005 by Glenn Leitz
All rights reserved.

Printed in the United States of America.

Library of Congress Cataloging-in-Publication Data

Long ago in the northern Palouse : an anthology of pioneer people, places, and events / compiled and edited by Glenn Leitz.
p. cm.
Includes bibliographical references and index.
ISBN-13: 978-0-922993-34-5 (pbk. : alk. paper)
ISBN-10: 0-922993-34-3 (pbk. : alk. paper)
1. Palouse River Valley (Idaho and Wash.)--History.
2. Frontier and pioneer life--Palouse River Valley (Idaho and Wash.)
I. Leitz, Glenn, 1930-
F897.P24L66 2005
979.7'39--dc22

2005022613

Marquette Books
3107 E. 62nd Ave.
Spokane, WA 99223
509-443-7057
books@marquettebooks.org
www.MarquetteBooks.org

This building was the original City Hall in Fairfield built about 1912. Used as fire station till 1977, now as Fairfield Museum since 1978.

Dedicated to
The Southeast Spokane County Historical Society

Proceeds from this book will promote area historical preservation

Table of Contents

Introduction and Acknowledgements — Page 1

Chapter 1 Reemphasizing Area History — Page 2

Chapter 2 Palouse Country Indians — Page 13

Chapter 3 The Wagon Train Pioneers — Page 24

Chapter 4 The Wild West — Page 38

Chapter 5 Maps That Connect Area History — Page 46

Chapter 6 Early Travel — Page 57

Chapter 7 Promoting the Palouse Region — Page 72

Chapter 8 Almost Forgotten Places — Page 81

Chapter 9 Historic Birds and Animals — Page 91

Chapter 10 Old Newspaper Stories — Page 98

Chapter 11 Local Pioneer Stories — Page 112

Epilogue — Page 131

Bibliography — Page 135

Index — Page 138

Introduction and Acknowledgements

The origin and inspiration for this history project was a variety of stories and newspaper articles that appeared in the early 1950's as a commemoration of the Washington Territorial Centennial of 1853. A little later in the 1960's, some of our area towns put together "community histories." These projects added a wealth of additional stories and information about the pioneer era. Now we can also add some more recently written "pioneer stories" that have appeared in current publications like the Palouse Magazine. All of these are still effectively keeping us connected to our area's past and give us some guidance as to who we are as individuals and also who we are as a community.

It is a somber fact that pioneer history has a tendency to grow dim with the passage of time. Now we are in a time frame another fifty years further down the road from the date of the territorial centennial. Remembering that sort of milestone gives us an excellent opportunity for another review and another look at local history. It also gives us another opportunity to remember that these stories are an affirmation of our heritage. A heritage bequeathed to us by the pioneers in this special part of the northern Palouse.

Fortunately there has been a core of people who have diligently put time and effort into preserving our local history for many years now. The local territorial centennial observance depended heavily on local people like Elizabeth Marion, Herb Stevens and Glen Adams. They contributed their own writings and helped garner many of the stories and interviews of that period from the area's pioneers, who, at that point, were the last generation that directly connected to the pioneer era. These direct contacts to pioneer times were very soon to disappear.

Today, members of the local historical societies still work to continue those efforts and preserve these stories. A special thank you is directed to Bernice Ostheller, who had a primary role in preserving a collection of the 1953 era articles and stories. This book's author/editor, Glenn Leitz, is busy researching and writing about area history. Many of his stories will be included as examples of recent efforts to add to and popularize Palouse country history.

CHAPTER 1

Reemphasizing Area History

Hangman Creek—A Lifeline To History In The Northern Palouse

The northern Palouse has a multi-faceted topography that makes it a unique and special place. Its vista of rolling dune-like hills, its well watered, rich volcanic soil, combine with seasonal changes that create a vibrant backdrop of spectacular colors. This makes it a place of very special beauty. That beauty inspires a special and deep affection among those of us who live within its borders.

Part of the identity of this region is also formed by other topographical features that make this area special. One of these important features is Hangman Creek. The very name has a stark and special cachet! Our stories start with this landmark as both a beginning and an ending to these tales.

Elizabeth Marion crafted a four part series of historical connections to our area's territorial centennial history. They appeared in 1953 in an area weekly. She designed that analysis of local history around our local stream. This series will serve as both an introduction and a conclusion to this book, bookends if you will, for this look at our history.

Hangman Creek By Elizabeth Marion

The biggest events and the important names and faces make the boldest stories and the biggest celebrations. But every area and locale has its own contributions to make to the whole of the events.

In its winding neighbor, Hangman Creek is a little highway of time, linking the long ago with today and tomorrow. A few of the important people and events are caught in that linking; but just as important in that total picture are the stoic unheroic builders of the regions that belong in the neighborhoods of this ancient stream. A stream whose very name is a small contribution to the everyday tongue and the history it tells.

Hangman Creek rises on the high slopes of the watershed east of Sanders in Idaho's Benewah County, in deep timber so tall and thick that the woods-flowers of the spring bear white blooms to make themselves seen in the green light. In its geographical beginning it is a mountain stream, clear and fast. It remained so for many years after its downhill haste took it into the written record of history. In the spring of 1806 when Lewis and Clark, camped on the Clearwater miles away to the south, they heard of it from area Indians going by. Their information was good, and Clark put it on his map with a fair degree of accuracy.

David Thompson was another very special early explorer. He was a Canadian, who in 1810 built Spokane House, the first white man's settlement in Washington. Thompson's journeys on his own map are incredible, even now; but when he was done he knew all about "the northwest," which in his day was no small place but a great circle enclosing Winnipeg and the Hudson's Bay forts beyond, the northern plains and the gigantic trough between the Rockies and the Cascades and all the great rivers herein, going east to the Mississippi basin and west down to the sea, at Astoria and the northern Vancouver. In that vastness, Thompson knew where Hangman Creek is, and put it down on his maps.

In the years after, the thin company of wilderness men knew where it was, and placed themselves on the Spokane River by the number of miles above or below the mouth of Hangman Creek, where then the Indians camped to fish for trout and salmon in the bright untamed waters of both streams. In time, when the sparse traffic made trails, the trails crossed Hangman, most of them near its mouth where they joined the main road along the river to and from Spokane House and the forts east and north. Only the Kentuck Trail bore off to the east, arriving at Spokane Bridge for its junction with the east-west road. The Kentuck Trail came by way of the towns in this neighborhood of ours—Rosalia, Waverly, through Big Flat (Bull Flat), Smythe's Ford, and still northeast through Mount Hope and Freeman, close by Mica and curving around the north ends of Saltese and Liberty lakes to its final goal at old Spokane Bridge.

In more experienced worlds than ours, some few people have noted that it appears to be true that if you have enough soldiers moving around, you will soon have a war moving around with them. This dismal game of cause and effect happened here in the fall of 1858, when the Indians and Wright's troops fought through the Palouse country down to the Spokane River and eastward through the valley till the Indians were beaten and all their transportation denied them by the doughty colonel, who ought to be known as the biggest horse thief in history. Having executed this brutal bit of strategy and almost a thousand horses, Wright held two councils, one at the Cataldo mission, and the second on Hangman Creek which was about to earn its popular name. There, near Smythe's Ford where the creek twists gently through meadow flats and woods that smell of balm-of-Gilead leaves and pine and fir, where in late September the aspens are gold and the elderberries heavy with grape-blue crop, the troops camped for five days and the Spokanes and their friends—the Colvilles, Pend Oreilles, even a few Coeur d'Alenes who had missed the first dose of humiliation—came to that sort of council which falls to the vanquished.

The troublesome Yakima, Qualchan, was decoyed in to the council and hanged within 15 minutes of his appearance on September 24. In the evening of the next day a company of Palouses came, and six of those stayed, because they were also dead. That was the day Lt. Mullan returned to camp with the recovered howitzers and the dead soldiers of the Steptoe battle; and the next day all the warriors, red and white, went away with their dead and their belligerences and left the creek to its autumn habits, to the deep-voiced winds which make a darker music in the woods there than anywhere

3

else along the creek, and to wait, perhaps, for the coming of the elusive man Smythe whose name clings to the ford.

Nobody knows when he came. He could not have been there in 1858 when the warriors' council was held; at least he is not mentioned in Wright's or Mullan's or Kip's accounts of the place. The next summer, Mullan camped there again, and does not mention him. But 12 years later, in 1872, a man describing the Kentuck Trail, calls the Hangman creek crossing Smythe's crossing, nobody else's. Ten years later, by 1882, Smythe had been and come and gone away again—some people say he simply vanished and left his horse to wander in the hills beyond the woods. Why should a shy lone man in those days go off without his transportation? But nobody knows for sure when he came, or where he went or why, or even whether he left his bones where his name is to this day.

By the 60's, traffic was heavy on the trails and crossings of the creek. Emigrants going south into the promised land of Walla Walla and the Willamette passed through the Palouse without noticing it except as another obstacle between them and their goal; and the miners going northeast into the Blackfoot mining country in Montana used the Palouse for passage way. Emigrants and miners and their followers—"by the thousands," the new territory's legislature was told when being asked for a bridge here, a ferry there, a grant for this and a grant for that; and few of them lingered on their going—the census of 1870 could only find 147 noses to count in all of Spokane and Whitman counties. In the next ten years the gold wore out and the Palouse began to look useful and the 1880 census recorded 11,276 people in the same area.

After a due time in history passed; after the mountain men, the miners and the soldiers had seen the creek, another group of men came on the scene. The Jesuit priests first began a primitive mission on the St. Joseph (St. Joe) River. Then yearly floods pushed them on to Cataldo. Here the rising tide of miners and immigrants created conflicts and "bad influences" and the Fathers moved their church, their work and their Indians into the mission valley of DeSmet. This was some distance upstream from that fateful crossing where Father Joset had been a witness to the Indian surrender at the council at Smythe's Ford.

Joset had struggled through all the difficulties and miseries of the wars of 1858 in the role of an envoy or "go between." He had also worked with the other great men of his order, Fathers Point, Ravalli, and DeSmet—Father Joset died at the mission in 1899.

By the time the Fathers came to Chief Seltice's valley of the creek, there was already the beginning of a town at Latah, which owns a little footnote in the geology books because the bones of a prehistoric mammoth were found there in 1878; in 1879 a post office at A.D. Thayer's place presaged the birth of Waverly a little way downstream. There was Tekoa, with the Biblical name and the railroads and the Whitman county hills to feed it.

Waverly is the town that used to leap back and forth across Hangman with the agility of a grasshopper; nowadays it is back where it started, and fairly meek about it after a hectic career. At the turn of the century, and on the town's first leap over the

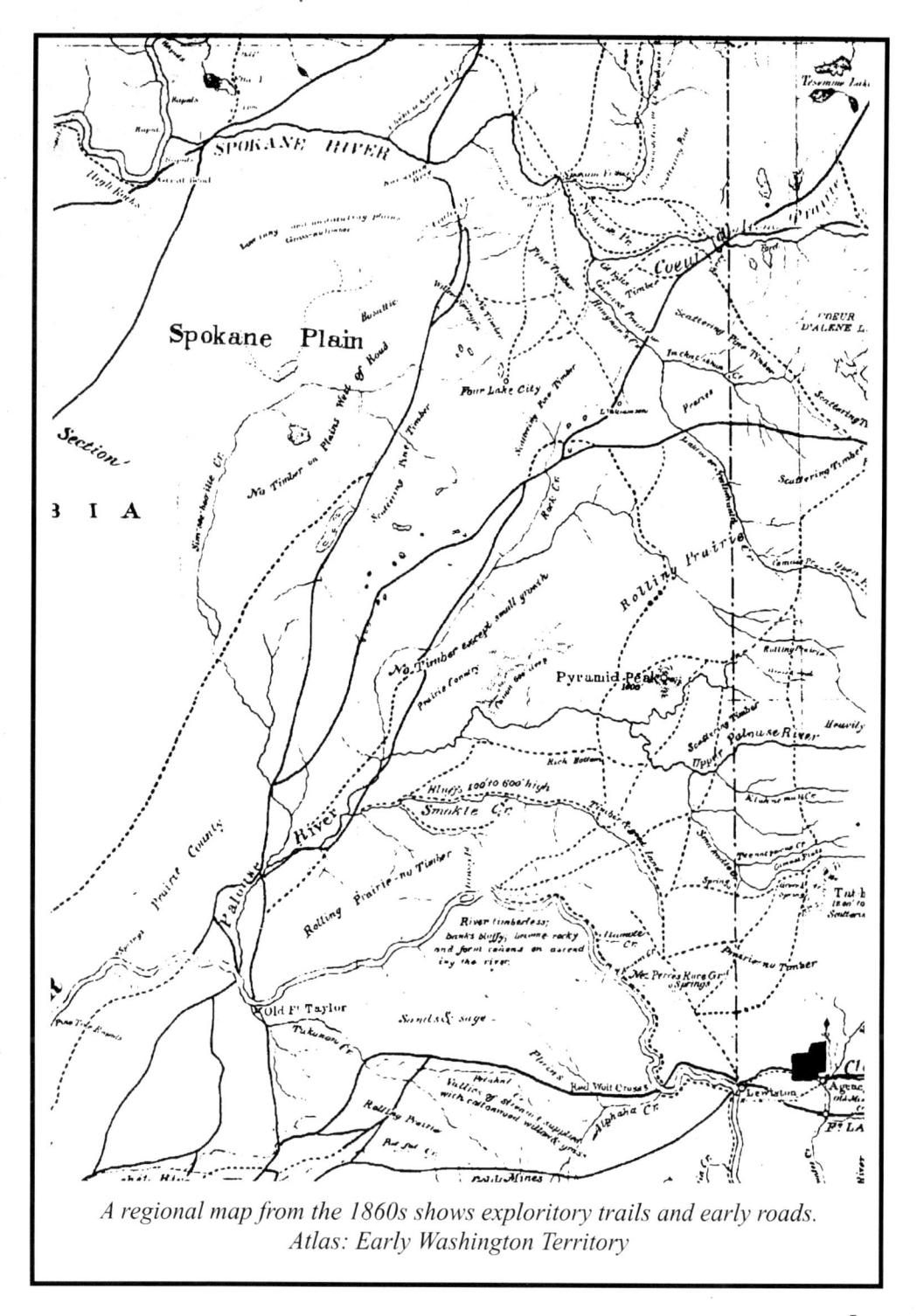

*A regional map from the 1860s shows exploritory trails and early roads.
Atlas: Early Washington Territory*

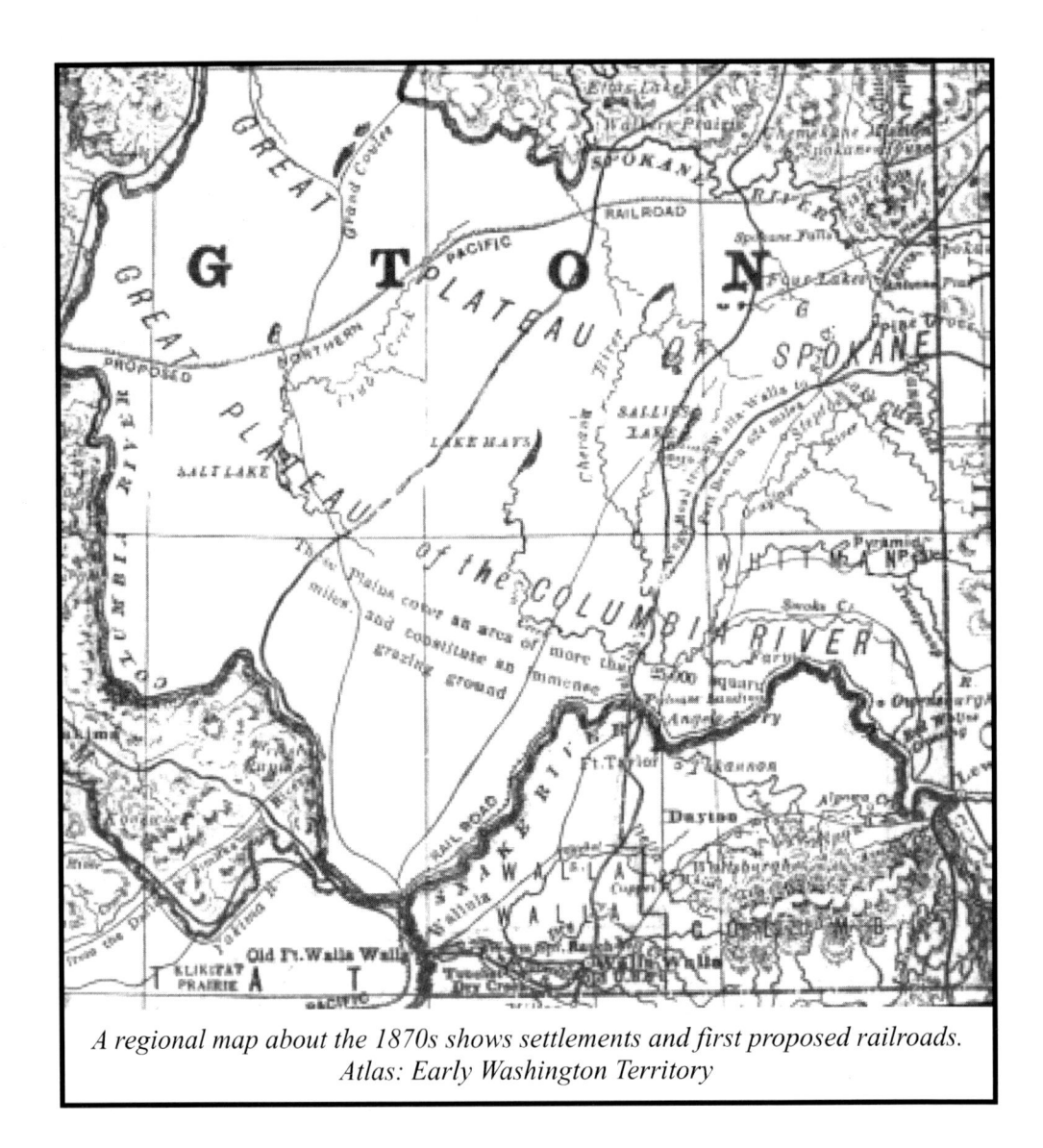

A regional map about the 1870s shows settlements and first proposed railroads.
Atlas: Early Washington Territory

creek, there was a sugar beet factory and half a million dollar's worth of work and money invested in an enterprise that crumbled into oblivion, leaving behind it a little history brightened by that spurt of prosperity from the lowly beet, and by all manner of fine past things: a flood once when the factory's crib dam burst, an electric railroad which boasted a division point at Spring Valley, a flashy baseball team, a newspaper frothing with municipal pride, a murder never solved to this day, and busy streets that knew, among other people, Japanese crews who worked in the beet fields and Italian crews who worked for awhile on that curious project, the roadbed glorified by the name of the North Coast railroad.

In the inland west, mysterious railroads were almost as numerous as those shy people like Smythe who are always there just ahead of the first pioneers. Some sections of it are still plain, though pines grow 100 feet high atop them and the mock orange and the thorn brush thrive; but the mysterious railroad never came. They tore down Waverly's beet factory and its dream, and the town leaped back across the creek to catch onto a shift in the highway. Joe Henry's mill is gone, though it stood dark and deserted, sturdy as the man who built it, long after he was dead; the size of its beams and the stoutness of its footing attesting to the character of the builder.

Editor's note *We will briefly revisit the conclusion of Elizabeth Marion's sketches at the end of this book. For now, let us go on to some of the other events and stories that tell the history of the northern Palouse. These stories will unfold in a somewhat chronological sequence.*

Connecting The Geology, Geography And History Of The Palouse

Geology, geography and history often have a common denominator. We live in a region where these three subjects combine in a particularly interesting way.

People do not usually give too much thought to the landscapes around them that they see day to day. These landscapes in our own area have a uniqueness that we have just begun to understand in the lifetime of today's citizens. These features trace back to the lava flows and glacial flooding that occurred long, long years ago.

Beginning sometime after the lava flows ended, a cover of wind-blown silt or loess began to accumulate over the lava fields, eventually producing the fertile soils of eastern Washington. This loess was largely made up of the volcanic ash that blew in from the volcanoes that are scattered among the Cascade Mountains of Washington and Oregon. Thus, before the onset of the "Great Flood," the geologic setting of the region was a thick, tilted saucer of basalt, in places warped into massive mounds and ridges. This was completely overlain with "frosting" of loess.

How did the region look if one were standing atop Steptoe Butte eons ago? The view in any direction would be beautifully rolling grassland speckled with roaming exotic animals. Gigantic deer, antelope and bison were among the examples of the grass eaters. Primitive horses and camels would roam freely; they would become extinct, but modern time's man would re-introduce them. (Yes, even the camel returned briefly in the heyday of mining pack trains.) Primitive and immense wolves, bear and saber-tooth cats led the ranks of the carnivores. Even stranger animals like giant sloth, huge beavers and lumbering mastodons and mammoths passed across the stage of time.

Yet in the distance, the Cascades and the Rockies formed hazy blue backdrops to the east and west, not unlike what we see today. This tranquil scene would become the setting for coming catastrophes.

We see numerous references to these events in what is referred to as the creation of the "channeled scablands" by huge floods of melting glacial waters. We now understand that this post-glacial flooding occurred over and over (maybe as many as 100 different events). Also, the intensity of these floods varied somewhat with some being more catastrophic in their volume of water and duration. The glaciers might advance about as far south as the Spokane Valley and then, in a warming cycle, retreat back to the north. When the glaciers would retreat, huge lakes of dammed up water would break loose releasing huge amounts of floodwater. These events could produce deluges of water that could surpass by ten times all the flow of the present-day rivers of the world. This type of flooding has never occurred anywhere else in the history of the world!

An understanding of these events and their effect on our region did not come about until the 1920s. A young geology graduate named J. Harland Bretz graduated from the University of Chicago and then came out to the Inland Northwest. He was intrigued with the region, and he puzzled

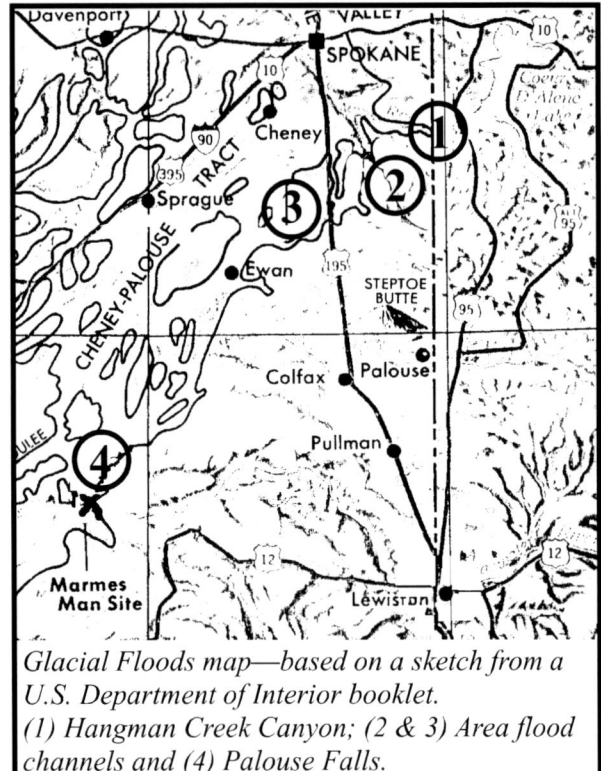

Glacial Floods map—based on a sketch from a U.S. Department of Interior booklet.
(1) Hangman Creek Canyon; (2 & 3) Area flood channels and (4) Palouse Falls.

over the peculiar and unusual geology and geography. He came to the conclusion that some catastrophic flooding event was the primary force in shaping the region's features.

This flew in the face of the old "slow evolutionary change" doctrines that were the basis of the science of geology at that time. Few arguments get more heated than when professors and scientists get challenged on some of their long held theories. Bretz was at the center of a raging controversy for years. Before too long, high-level aerial photography came into vogue. With this, and other, information a newer group of more open-minded geologists swung over to Bretz' ideas, and soon the disagreements trailed off. Since then "catastrophic events" have become recognized as an important shaper of worldwide geography.

Landscape Features In The Palouse

Here in the northern Palouse we readily recognize that features like Coeur d'Alene Lake to the northeast and the "potholes" and lakes just to the west are the results of that post-glacial activity. We may be a little less aware of some of the other equally interesting local geography right in our own back yards. The rugged basalt canyon where Rock Creek and Hangman Creek merge is the result of a huge outflow of glacial water from lower Coeur d'Alene Lake. These local floodwaters surged from Windy Bay, across to Rock Creek through the Rockford area and on to the Hangman Valley.

I have frequently surprised people by asking them if they realize that the "flat" just east of Liberty School (midway between Spangle and Waverly) is one of the easternmost of the glacial floodways. This may be more easily observed if you note the geology at North Pine, three miles north of Rosalia. Two channels merged and then poured a deluge of water into Pine Creek where Highway 195 crosses today. In the post-glacial period this was part of the flood of water that scoured out the Rock Lake, Hole-in-the-Ground, Bonnie Lake complex that most of us in this region know very well.

Some other points of interest a little farther away would be the fact that these floods backed up a lake of water up the Snake River at Lewiston to the depth of 600 feet. The dramatic geology at the Palouse Falls site is another premiere example of these exceptional events.

A Current Development - There is a large-scale effort today to promote the dramatic and unique geology of this region into a major tourism project. Initial studies have laid out quite a comprehensive proposal for bicycle and hiking trails, interpretive signs, self-guided auto tours and large-scale publicity efforts. Funding is being sought by a variety of local groups and organizations dedicated to advancing an awareness of these uniquely interesting features of our regional scene.

Boundaries Of The Palouse

Setting the boundaries of the Palouse region has always seemed to generate a variety of questions and debates. At different times the Palouse region has either shrunk or expanded, depending on what reporter or analyst was being heard. This situation may be even more confusing in trying to outline the borders of the northern Palouse.

The eastern and northern borders of this region seemingly should be easy to place. Features like Brown's Mountain and Mica Peak are notable landmarks to the north. The foothills of the Bitterroots create a reference line on the east. Still, questions quickly arise as to how to include valleys and farming areas that extend almost to Coeur d'Alene Lake.

Then we come to real confusion with regard to the boundary on the west. The more common guidelines say the Palouse extends west to the "channeled scablands," referring to these profiles of the glacial flooding in the region. These features exist almost as far as Waverly and Rosalia, and Spangle sits immediately adjacent to major flood channels. The northern Palouse obviously encompasses an area considerably farther to the west.

I have asked many people where they would place the western edge of the Palouse. The question is almost always met with a puzzled look or rambling comments. If there is any consensus at all, it would be that the western edge of the entire Palouse region is a wavering line from about Cheney all the way down to the southeast corner of Whitman County.

The southern boundary for the region emphasized in this book is a somewhat arbitrary decision on my part. A line across northern Whitman County and specifically the Pine Creek watershed seem to be a reasonable choice. Farmington on the east and the Bonnie Lake-Rock Lake area on the west will suffice as southern cornerstones.

Streams In The Northern Palouse

Hangman Creek

The northern Palouse region can be further defined by considering the course and boundaries of the area's streams. Hangman Creek is the largest stream, and it is a central feature in almost all texts and descriptions of the northern Palouse.

Hangman Creek has a number of interesting geological features that have received surprisingly little attention. For a considerable part of its course the southern watershed boundary is only a few short miles from the main channel. The ancient geologic "uplifting" of the area pushed the course of the stream northeastward until the stream runs right up to the base of Tekoa Mountain and then downstream near Waverly it had the same effect at the Waverly Butte, which is the westernmost extension of the Bitterroot Mountain Range.

Downstream from Waverly the huge volumes of glacial floodwaters flattened the southern border of the watershed in the primary flood channels (Liberty School and Spangle areas) so that the watershed divide is almost indiscernible.

A second important watershed feature is that the Hangman Creek channel directly follows the "Latah Earthquake Fault." The normal inclination might be to ask how a crooked, meandering stream that appears to be wandering at will could be following a fault line. Current use of high-altitude mapping and photos from space show a surprisingly straight trajectory for the stream's path, from the Tekoa-Tensed area to its intersection with the Spokane River. Recent earthquake shocks in the Spokane area have brought a resurgence of interest and awareness of this phenomenon.

Pine Creek

The second largest stream in this area of the Palouse is Pine Creek. Just how much of the northern Palouse this stream drains could be subject to a debate. For this particular book we will be considering an area from about Farmington to Pine City. Early exploration and military maps used the Indian name In-gossomen for this stream, and that name persisted up to settlement times. Farmington, one of the very earliest towns in this part of the Palouse and near the stream's headwaters, was first called Pine Creek. When it was platted as Farmington the original name seemed to pass to the stream.

While not as bold and brassy as Hangman Creek to the north, Pine Creek still has an important place in local history. Col. Steptoe's ill-starred command rode to their rendezvous with destiny along its banks. Then near Rosalia, one of the most important pioneer mammoth finds turned up in the 1870s. Today, one of the region's premier landmarks straddles Pine Creek valley—the great concrete arched bridge at Rosalia is another sentinel of a dramatic past.

Another point of interest with these two streams is that Hangman Creek waters drain north to the Spokane River and then into the Columbia River. Pine Creek flows south to the Palouse, then to the Snake River and on to the Columbia.

Two Rock Creeks

Another peculiar situation exists in the north Palouse, in that there are tributary streams of both Hangman and Pine Creek that are called Rock Creek. Needless to say, this causes some misunderstandings. In some instances I will designate them Rock Creek One and Rock Creek Two in an effort to avoid confusion.

Rock Creek One drains a large area east of Fairfield all the way to the Plummer and Worley areas. Then it turns west through Rockford and drains down into a deep, scenic canyon, where it meets Hangman Creek not far from the old ghost town of Duncan.

Rock Creek Two drains an area west of Spangle over toward the Turnbull Game Refuge. The water then runs south through the Chapman-Bonnie Lake area, through the Hole-in-the-Ground and into Rock Lake. Much of Rock Creek Two's main channel is through a rugged basalt region that is little changed over eons of time.

It is easy to understand why these streams are such a terrific focus and reference for many of these stories of northern Palouse history.

Smythe's Ford - An Example Of The Secrets Of Yesteryear

The Palouse region has a multitude of historic places where various organizations have erected monuments to commemorate special events. Today these markers can still stimulate our interest and attention and reacquaint us with important aspects of our region's history.

The Smythe's Ford Historic Site is located on Hangman Creek about 20 miles south of Spokane. In pre-settlement times Hangman Creek ran a much larger volume of water than it does today. Accordingly, for much of the year a good ford or crossing site was an important geographic location.

For untold eons of time this place was crucial to the area's Native Americans. As they traveled the region on their food gathering and trading routes, this was a common meeting place, as both north-south and east-west trails crossed here. These Indian trails became the first roads for the white explorers, traders and military, and the fording site became a landmark to note on their early maps.

As time and history moved on, settlement soon began. It was at this time that the site effectively became known on maps and travel journals as Smythe's Ford. This name commemorates the first white man to live here. Smythe was apparently a trapper or a trader in the interval between the Indian wars and the start of permanent white settlement.

Smythe is only remembered as a "sliding, unsocial character" who left no records of his stay here. He is one of those intriguing historical mysteries. As Elizabeth Marion noted, when Smythe dropped out of sight, his horse was reported to be seen unattended, grazing on the nearby hills. It would be unusual for him to abandon his horse—Did he meet with foul play? This only adds a final question mark to the mystery!

Additional stories at this location revolve around the development of important pioneer roads. The building of the Mullan Road, officially the Walla Walla to Fort Benton Military Road, began in 1859. This is probably the best known route in our region.

The other pioneer road to come to this crossing on Hangman Creek was the Kentuck Trail. It was somewhat less significant than the Mullan Road, but it lasted for a longer period of time. The Kentuck Trail was the easternmost and shortest route from the Walla Walla country to this region's first transportation hub—Spokane Bridge. More details about these two roads will appear later.

By the early 1900s traffic and progress had bypassed Smythe's Ford, and it became a quiet rural byway. But it was still to have one final event of note. In the early decades of the twentieth century local people saw the need to preserve our area's pioneer heritage, and they were instrumental in placing the granite monument that marks this historic spot. That monument's testimony helps us to note the passage of time and history at this very special place.

Summary

Geology and geography have combined in a particularly significant way in our region. Many factors involved in developing area resources, the first roads and transportation routes and how settlement proceeded all combined to characterize the uniqueness of this particular area.

Finally, this does all have a relationship to regional history. The travel and migration routes of the Indians were directly tied to this geography. These trails became, in turn, the travel routes of the white man. These old trails and roads have a particular fascination of their own, as well as many stories to tell.

CHAPTER 2

Palouse Country Indians

Introduction

Almost all of us have some degree of interest in the Indians who occupied this area. For thousands of years they lived on this land, developing a culture and a way of life that served them well. With the appearance of the white man that way of life passed from the scene in a comparative blink of an eye. The Indian population was never large by current standards, but today it has almost disappeared. Only in the very northeastern corner of the Palouse—on the Coeur d'Alene Reservation in the Tensed, Plummer and Worley (Idaho) area—is the Native American still a significant presence.

There Were Originally Three Tribes in the Region

The Palouse, the Coeur d'Alenes and the Spokanes are the tribes with the most direct connection to our region. The Palouse tribe presence was the most wide-ranging, while the Coeur d'Alene and Spokane presence was basically in the northern part of the region. Interestingly, these three tribes co-mingled in the upper Hangman Creek drainage. During the root digging they would gather annually to socialize and catch up on regional news and gossip. These events were an occasion for trading, feasting, gambling, inter-clan and inter-tribal marriages and alliances; and about every other kind of social interaction.

Root digging grounds often seemed to be viewed as a common

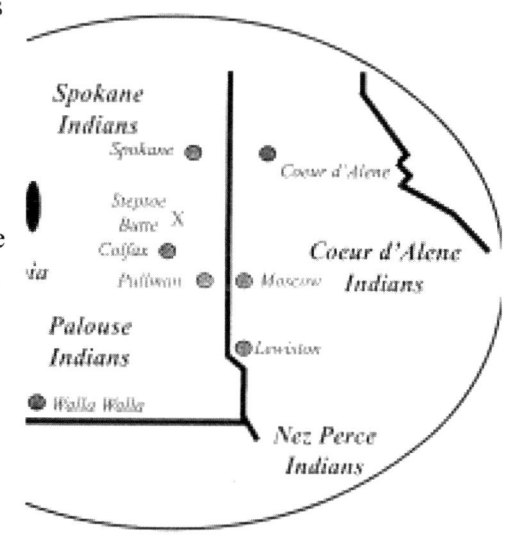

resource and were somewhat exempt from claims of tribal ownership. The fact that root digging grounds were physically improved by the tilling of the digging process was quite likely a factor. At any rate the upper Hangman Valley seems to be especially noteworthy as a meeting ground for these three tribes.

Some of the most interesting regional Indian history began with the Palouse tribe. It is probably another good starting point to consider briefly where the name "Palouse" originated. This is another question that has generated quite a bit of controversy. One argument supports the opinion that "Palouse" is a word of French origin that describes features of grassland. Grasslands are certainly a prominent hallmark. The other basic argument is that early explorers found Indians, that in numerous variations were called something like Palus, Pelushes, Paloosha, etc. This seemed to be based on the fact that these peoples' main village was at the mouth of the region's main tributary to the Snake River. This village was called Palus because of a large rock formation that had an important place in Indian mythology. This provided an unchanging place name in the region. Early explorers and traders in the region seemed to make that the basis for using the Palouse name on their first maps.

The first explorers estimated the Palouse at about 500 people. There was a surprising difference in population estimates depending on the source. An important factor was that the Indian population began to be affected almost immediately by diseases the white man introduced. The consequences were almost unbelievable. The Indian population was decimated...in many villages half or more of the population died. In the worst scenarios there might not be any survivors.

Manifest Destiny

A chilling example of what shaped white man practice in dealing with the Indians was the doctrine of "Manifest Destiny." The politicians and military men, and most of the rest of the population, felt the United States had a God given right to occupy the North American continent to the shore of the Pacific Ocean. Nothing was to be allowed to stand in the way of that goal. If the Indians were an obstruction they needed to be moved out of the way—whatever that required would be done!

Conflict Looms

The details of the Indian wars in this area in the 1850's are too complex to detail here and they have been well covered by numerous accounts. But less well known and understood is the unique role of the Palouse Indians in these hostilities.

The Palouse Indians were in the forefront of almost all of the regional hostilities, starting with the Whitman Massacre in 1847, through the Gov. Isaac Stevens' Walla Walla treaties of 1855-56 and the conflicts that it set off in the Walla Walla and Yakima regions, then on to the 1858 campaigns of Steptoe and Wright, the Palouse were in the thick of it all. Little wonder they became known as troublemakers and renegades! Then when Col. Wright made post battle treaties with the rest of the tribes, he refused to treaty with the Palouse. They were to be on the strictest of probation—one more incident and Wright promised he would wipe them out "every man, woman and child."

The Palouse Indian Destiny

The Palouse Indians never received a reservation of their own. The tribes' remnants have been scattered to a number of northwestern reservations dominated by other tribes. Today there is a relative handful of Indians that still try to maintain a "Palouse identity." Their situation is quite precarious.

In today's language we use the word "patriot" to describe people who love their homeland and make every effort and every sacrifice to preserve that bond. The Palouse Indians were instead given the name "outlaws and renegades." History has many ironies! I am reminded of some phrases displayed at the Oregon Trail Interpretive Center near Baker City, Oregon:

Epilogue for the Palouse Indians

"The ashen faced strangers came to our land. They brought things like brass kettles, brightly colored beads, firearms, matches, and cotton and wool clothing. They were clever but not wise. They upset everything! They dug for gold and muddied the water. They turned over the meadows and destroyed the camas. The "people," the Indians, grew ill and died. The newcomers made war. The treaties of the great Walla Walla Council of 1855 promised protection but the miners and the settlers took what they wanted. The times were bitter—like winter when there is no more food. The world fell to pieces."

Soon a way of life that had existed for uncounted centuries was gone!

The Coeur d'Alene Indian Tribe

In the 1860's and 70's most of the Coeur d'Alene Indians were living in a corridor from Cataldo on the east, along the northern edge of Coeur d'Alene Lake and also around Hayden Lake, and then west along the Spokane River as far as Liberty Lake.

Here they began a major conversion to farming and a considerable curtailment of their nomadic lifestyle. At the same time this corridor was becoming a primary route for travel and activity by the increasing white population. This was an ongoing source of friction and problems. The whites were a considerable corrupting influence on Indian morals and there was an ongoing effort to inappropriately acquire Indian property and land.

The Jesuit missionaries recognized this situation would only get worse and they began to cast an eye toward the productive lands at the south end of the Coeur d'Alene region in the Tekoa-Tensed area. At first the Indians' attachment to the familiar surroundings where they were living was unyielding, but the priests were even more unbending. Over a period of several years they turned much energy into effecting this move. In the end they were successful and the Sacred Heart Mission and the center of tribal activity was shifted to the new location at DeSmet.

Here the rich soil provided an exceptional farming and ranching opportunity. Numerous Indian families developed farms of 1,000 acres or more. Annual inspections from the Bureau of Indian Affairs at Washington, D.C., proudly proclaimed that the Coeur d'Alenes were one of the most successful examples of a conversion to reservation life.

Politics and the Reservation

Over a long period of time there were many arguments about the reservation size and the location of permanent boundaries. Indian leaders and their representatives made many trips to Washington, D.C., to lobby Congress and government bureaucrats for a favorable resolution of this matter.

Chief Andrew Seltice was the head Coeur d'Alene chief at this time. (The Saltese area in the Spokane Valley and the railroad junction/grain storage site between Tekoa and Farmington—although spelled differently—are Seltice namesakes.) Steven Liberty, who gave his name to Liberty Lake, and Lewis Peone (of Peone Prairie northeast of Spokane)—were examples of other Indian leaders who traveled to the east to present the Indian case. However, by the 1880's, the reservation was cut down to the present boundaries and 345,000 acres. Some additional financial payments and some services for the Indians were part of this settlement.

Most of the white population and their government representatives felt the land promises were far beyond the Indian needs. Finally in the early 1900's the government decided that the Indians should individually receive 160-acre allotments and some additional land for hunting, timber, etc., should be held jointly in tribal ownership. The rest should be opened up to homesteading, by a lottery drawing, to anyone who wanted to sign up for a 160-acre homestead.

Over a period of years this resulted in almost unbelievable change. For a number of complex and somewhat hard to understand reasons, Indian farming operations changed drastically. Before long many Indian allotments shifted to operation by whites. A long period of Indian poverty and social stagnation occurred.

More About the Mission School and Church

In this same time period there was a very important development at DeSmet with the establishment of a major school system. The Catholic priests and sisters were at the center of a large parochial boarding school with a number of impressive buildings where the Indian children were educated. A typical but unhappy note of this schooling effort was the strong desire to minimize the Indian culture and language. This was supposedly done to help the Indians adapt to a new and better lifestyle, but the dysfunctional effects on Indian family life and culture were serious and long lasting.

One of the landmarks of the mission at this time was an imposing gothic style wooden church. The high multi-windowed gables and the spires and ornate woodworking of the church front were very distinctive. Inside the church was highlighted with a grand, gothic style altar and the typical tall pulpit and statuary of the early 1900's.

A Coeur d'Alene elder named Agatha Timothy, perhaps 100 years old or more, told her younger contemporaries that she loved this church so much that she would take this beautiful building with her when she went to heaven. The day after she died, in April 1939, the church burned to the ground.

Early Day Business Activity With the Indians

Indian trade and business were very important to pioneer towns along the Washington-Idaho border. There was hardly any development of towns on the reservation until the private ownership of property began in 1910. The towns of Rockford, Fairfield, Tekoa and Farmington were where much of the business activity took place and this continued to be very important for several more decades.

Many newspaper accounts and historic commentaries mention this importance of the Indian trade to the local economies. Often these accounts tell that it was common for business men to declare that their Indian customers were to be noted for their honesty and reliability in settling their accounts.

Another business related story is that when tribal boundaries and land ownership changes were made in treaty negotiations there could be considerable cash settlements to the Indians for ceded lands. In 1892 the government bought the northern part of the reservation for $550,000. Every man, woman and child was said to receive $1,130.00. An old Rockford area newspaper (1892) shows a group of about a dozen Coeur d'Alene Indians who had come into a local bank to deposit a land settlement payment. This was a banner event for local banking interests and made front page headlines.

Some of our older citizens can still remember when Indian families would regularly come to area towns. In the 1930's some might still drive a buckboard or a buggy. The women typically wore colorful head scarves and the bright-eyed children would peek out at the strange sights with excitement and wonder.

Chief Andrew Seltice

Almost any account of the Coeur d'Alene tribe will include stories of perhaps their most notable tribal chief of pioneer times—Chief Andrew Seltice. In his youth he was involved in the infamous Steptoe Battle at Rosalia. Here area Indians handily defeated an out gunned army unit. Then shortly later he experienced the vengeance wreaked on the Indians by Col. George Wright's punitive campaign. This experience evidently led to a lifelong understanding that the Indians had little chance of defending themselves against the U.S. Army's military might and that the Indians' only practical course was negotiation—as difficult as that might be.

Seltice went on to be a widely respected and important emissary for his people. Much of this respect came as a result of his efforts to be a peacekeeper.

When the first settlers came into this region in the 1870's there were several outbreaks of distant Indian hostilities. The nearest of these was the Nez Perce War of 1877. Seltice was a strong voice against any involvement by the Coeur d'Alenes. In fact he received wide commendation for having his people watch the settlers' farms and stock when panic would cause the whites to flee their scattered homes and seek safety.

Seltice also made a notable name for himself as a spokesperson and negotiator for tribal rights and reservation boundary claims disputes. He made many trips to Washington, D.C. Seltice was a tall, impressive looking man. He dressed in a suit and a trademark high silk hat, and he was treated with deference by Indians and whites alike.

One year at a special 4th of July celebration in Farmington he was an honored guest and gave an address to the crowd that attracted a great deal of favorable comment. The fact that he was so highly regarded in this sort of a setting is certainly noteworthy. It was also Seltice who refused to give up a drunken Indian to a white posse. The Indian was accused of murder. Seltice wouldn't give up the Indian until the posse punished the white man who sold him the liquor. Upon his death, newspapers across the region had extensive articles chronicling his many roles and accomplishments as an important Indian leader.

In a historical note in the Tekoa Standard Register (no date given) there was the following comment: Chief Seltice wore a high silk hat and drove a hearse to church, but he was decorated by the government for saving the lives of white settlers in the area when they were threatened by an Indian war. When the Nez Perce hostiles created wide panic and gear in the Palouse, Seltice was a firm and strong voice against involvement by the Coeur d'Alenes.

An Important Area Indian Family—
The Garry's of the Spokane Indian tribe

Chief Spokane Garry of the Spokane Indian Tribe was another important historical figure in the region. His life spanned most of the nineteenth century and coincided with the change from an area dominated by the Indians to an area dominated by the white man. Much turmoil and trouble was the hallmark of that transition and Garry and his family were unfortunate participants and witnesses to much of the chaos that occurred. He tried to stand up for Indian rights, but he was mainly ineffectual against the increasing domination of the white man. In 1892 he died in poverty near Spokane—stripped of his property and dignity. He was buried in a pauper's grave in the Greenwood Cemetery in west Spokane.

Because of government Indian policies, about 1900, some of the Spokane-area Indians were sent to the Coeur d'Alene reservation near Worley, Idaho. Spokane Garry's widow Nina and his daughter Nellie were among those sent to this location. Nina and Nellie were of the Presbyterian faith while the Coeur d'Alene Indians were of the Catholic faith. There was considerable friction between Protestants and

(Above) Indian encampment at Fairfield. (Southeast Spokane County Historical Society)

(Left) Circled left to right) Nellie Garry, Andrew Seltice and Spokane Garry. (Southeast Spokane County Historical Society)

(Above) Nellie (on her horse.) (Southeast Spokane County Historical Society photo.) (Right) Nellie and Lucy Garry. (Northwest History Room, Spokane City Library)

Catholics at this time and as a result the Garry women made a connection to the Presbyterian Church in Fairfield to maintain their lifelong religious affiliation. Because of this bond, they became quite well known in the Fairfield area. Nina Garry died in the early 1900's and was buried in the Fairfield Cemetery—also in a pauper's grave.

By the 1920's area people were starting to take more interest and pride in the region's history. The importance of Chief Spokane Garry's role in our regional history became more and more appreciated. After much work and effort by history conscious groups and individuals, it was decided to honor Chief Garry by moving his grave to a prominent place in Greenwood Cemetery and to erect an impressive granite marker with a text that noted the importance of the role he played in our region's history.

A little later it was decided that it would be fitting that his wife Nina be buried by his side. Accordingly, her remains were removed from the Fairfield Cemetery and interred in an adjoining grave at Spokane (June 1962). Her name was also chiseled onto the granite marker.

Nellie Garry's Story

Meanwhile Nellie Garry was destined to live an exciting and interesting life. It was also, in many ways a hard and difficult life. She lived in a time when Indian women stood mainly in the background and were given little notice. This would not be the style of Nellie Garry!

Nellie became quite an active presence in the Fairfield-Worley area. She became good friends with the Colonel Edward Morrison family. The Morrisons were Fairfield's most prominent family (see further details in Morrison story). In addition, Nellie was well known and well regarded by a large number of other area pioneer families.

Nellie received an "allotment" of 160 acres when the Coeur d'Alene reservation was divided into homesteads. It was located about halfway between Fairfield and Tekoa at the upper end of the Lovell Valley. Here she became the focal point and matriarch of her family.

In a 1916 interview she reviewed much of her family history. She told that Spokane Garry had nine children with two wives. Many of his children died; among the survivors were her and her half-sister Lucy. At that point Nellie had survived three husbands and had born eight children and most of them had died. Father Thomas Connolly of the Sacred Heart Mission at DeSmet, Idaho, has a rather primitive genealogy of early Garry family members. Even with this sketchy family tree and Nellie's 1916 interview there are difficulties in obtaining a clear picture of family relationships. Over time and through marriage the family became Catholic.

Nellie's surviving children were girls and she had a major concern that the Garry name would pass from the scene so she requested that her grandson Ignace be given the Garry name.

Ignace received at least some of his education in rural one-room schools in

Rock Creek Valley in Washington. He went on to become active in tribal affairs—rising to the level of a chief. He had a son who was to become an even more widely known Indian leader. Both Ignace and his son Joseph lived on the Lovell Valley allotment.

Joseph Garry also attended the local pioneer schools as a boy. He served in World War II and after further education and job experience he returned to the area and also became deeply involved with the tribal government. By this time the tribe was adopting a tribal council form of government to replace the hereditary chiefs. Joe worked up to the position of chairman of the tribal council; then he went on to be involved on a much wider scene in national organizations. He eventually became the president of the National Congress of American Indians. Later Joe Garry was also elected to the state legislature of Idaho. Joe has now passed away without any male heirs. The Garry name may now be at an end on the Coeur d'Alene reservation.

> **Note:** *Area historian John Fahey recently wrote a book about Joseph Garry and his life and experiences as an Indian leader. (see sources) It gives a good insight into how events have shaped Indian politics on the local and national scenes. This was Fahey's last book—he passed away in the summer of 2004.*

Returning to Nellie's Story

It should be noted that an interview with an historic individual in pioneer times was referred to as a "Statement." Nellie's statement (interview) was made at an encampment at Indian Canyon just west of Spokane. It was taken by historian William S. Lewis, and the date was in May of 1916. This camp was near the location of Spokane Garry's death. The "Statement" is a single-spaced, typed, three-page document. It is a little goldmine of information, but it actually just scrapes the surface of information we would like to know today.

Nellie tells of some of her father, Spokane Garry's, life experiences from his boyhood education at Winnipeg, Canada, to his return as a preacher and teacher to his people. Nellie relates that her own basic education was as one of her father's pupils. She says she was a "dull" student, in an interesting aside. She also relates numerous details about Spokane Garry's long record of attempting to negotiate with the settlers and the politicians in an effort to preserve Indian lands and Indian rights. In the end all of these efforts were ineffectual and he was driven from his own land and into destitute circumstances.

Nellie had an interesting way of approximating her age. The Indians paid little attention to birthdays. She said, "I was born ten years before the 'Big Fight' (1858)." The Big Fight which at this point was 56 years earlier, of course was a reference to the Indian battles with the forces of Col. George Wright. This was the dramatic Indian war that took place in the Spokane area.

Nellie lived in an eventful period of time with unbelievable change. As a daughter of one of the region's best known leaders, she was a witness to the changes that pushed her father and her family into destitute circumstances. A widely told story is that Nellie did laundry for white families during her father's last years. How

Nellie and her mother survived the years between Spokane Garry's death and then their early years on the Coeur d'Alene reservation is also something of a puzzle—quite possibly they were in a status as wards of the government.

Nellie lived into an active old age. In her later years she seemed to be a frequent traveler between the Spokane area and the Coeur d'Alene reservation where her descendents lived. She always expressed amazement at the large city that grew up where she had lived as a girl.

Nellie and her half sister, Lucy Garry, grew old together. (Lucy was believed to be at least five years older). Both were frequently said to have lived to eighty or more. However, Nellie's reference to her age in her "statement" would seem to reflect her living to approximately age 76 when she died in 1924. Nellie and Lucy both died within a six-month interval. They are buried at the St. Michael's Indian cemetery northeast of Worley, Idaho.

A final story about Nellie is found in old newspaper accounts about Nellie and Lucy being involved with a moving picture studio in Spokane. There were "Westerns" and other outdoor themed movies being made out at the Esmeralda area by a company that called itself the Minnehaha Studio. Nellie and Lucy were to be considered for "bit parts" in a cowboy and Indian epic. The editor has made some effort to determine whether such a movie was actually filmed, but no evidence has been found at this point. It may be destined to remain a mystery.

> **Note:** *Comments and pictures of Nellie Garry are fairly common but they are usually scattered and unconnected. I have never seen any real overview of her life, so it has been an interesting experience to make just a small effort in that direction. Nellie Garry has a special place in our region's pioneer history and she is one of my favorite individuals from the distant past. Nellie Garry became a notable figurehead for the Indian part of the regional history. She was a frequent guest participant at conventions and meetings. Dressed in Indian garb, giving a prayer in the Salish language or performing an Indian sage smoke ceremony, could be ways she would express Indian culture.*

It is easy to conclude the Garry family's involvement in the Indian life and history of this area makes them persons of a special and rare historical importance.

The Anasta Williams Affair

This Indian segment will close with a story on a light-hearted note. It is edited from an account Herb Stevens wrote for the Worley Community History of some years ago. This story tells of a series of events that occurred on the Coeur d'Alene reservation west of Worley, Idaho.

In the second decade of the 1900's road improvement was receiving some much needed attention on the route to Rockford. One of the property owners along the road was an Indian by the name of Anasta Williams. Williams had a first rate farm with an impressive set of buildings. In addition he had a well graveled one-half mile race track that was closely fenced inside and out.

Anasta had a passion for fast horses and on this track he exercised his runners and held many local horse races. Anasta objected to anything that might interfere with his race track and refused to give a right of way for the road project because the intended road was aligned to follow one side of his race course. Reluctant as he was, the road project proceeded anyway.

When the new road was made it ran right up to his race track from the east, entered the track through a wire gate, followed the track half way around, made its exit through another wire gate to continue on to Rockford, and of course in coming from Rockford this order was reversed—you entered from the west, turned left at the east side to continue on toward Worley. As you can see, this caused a great deal of gate opening, and gates were often left open, and this greatly increased Anasta's dissatisfaction. He often threatened to shoot trespassers, but no blood was ever spilled.

On the occasion of the 4th of July, 1916, two well known men of the Worley Community decided to attend the celebration being held in Rockford. They drove a team and buggy and made the trip to Rockford without incident. Fourth of July celebrations in those days can never be described as "dry" affairs—and for these two celebrants it was very "moist." After all day in Rockford and considerable celebrating, these men left in the late evening, for the return trip to Worley. It is said that by the time they reached the state line they were able to follow the road only because it was well fenced on both sides.

When they reached the entrance gate to Anasta's race track they had to stop and open the gate to go any farther. They entered the race track, but in the dark and in their existing state of inebriation they were not able to locate the exit gate. And it is probable that they were unable even to remember that such a gate existed. So they spent the rest of the night in an endless circling of the race track.

Several hours and many miles later, daylight found them still driving around Anasta's one-half mile race track. But time had also brought on a degree of sobriety and through the combination of sobering up and the coming of daylight came realization of the way they had spent the night.

They were able to regain the highway and urge their now tired team on to home. On this trip more miles were covered than on any other trip between the two towns.

The county was finally able to condemn this little bit of disputed right of way and the two ends of the new road were united. But it was a matter of indirect force and never voluntary on the part of old Anasta.

"When and if you travel this highway today, be thankful that you are not slowed up by two wire gates and a quarter of a mile of mud, dirt and gravel as was once the case."

CHAPTER 3

The Wagon Train Pioneers

A Young Girl Remembers The Wagon Trip West
And The First Settlers In The Palouse

Introduction

Vivid and detailed accounts of pioneer experiences dating back to the very first settlers coming into the Palouse region are of great interest to us today. This particular story begins with the unique focus of a six-year-old girl. She and her family made the long wagon trek across the western United States and then homesteaded near Latah. The extraordinary details of this girl's remembrances make this an unusual pioneer account.

Amanda Wimpy's Family

Amanda Wimpy's parents were part of an extended family clan that lived near the Missouri River on the Arkansas-Missouri border region. This area had divided sympathies in the Civil War. As a "border region" there was a dramatic divergence of support for one side or the other in this horrific conflict. Even after the war ended, local conflicts still created an atmosphere that seethed with enmity and turmoil. Another major factor of unease was the widespread health problems with malaria which was rampant here. Reasons to leave this venue seemed compelling.

One of the patriarchs of this family was a man called Richard H. Wimpy. He had achieved the rank of a Major in the North's army. As was the case with numerous Civil War officers, that honorific title was to be the preface for his name for the rest of his life. He was an intelligent and adventuresome man—these were qualities that would serve him well as he decided to strike out for a new life pioneering in a raw and distant land.

He was the advance scout for many family members as he arrived in the Pacific Northwest via the overland wagon trails in 1872. He then made his way north from the Walla Walla region all the way to the farthest edge of the frontier—a place called Hangman Creek. This stream and locale had acquired that somber title as a result of an Army-Indian war incident when seven Indians were hung nearby as retaliation for their objections to the white man's increasing incursions. This event had occurred eighteen years earlier. Now, finally, white settlement was ready to begin rolling over the region in a massive, undeterrable flood.

Wimpy was the first settler here. He liked the fertile, verdant region and he immediately relayed word back to his kinsmen that he had found an "area of great promise." Other family members were quick to follow.

Tom Wimpy, a younger brother, along with his wife and two daughters, began to plan their westward expedition to the far off Washington Territory. Mrs. Tom Wimpy's brother, John Anderson, with his wife and six-month-old son, would also join with them as they set off on this epic trip.

Amanda was only six years old on this journey, but her memories are surprisingly detailed and inclusive. Of the wagons, the livestock and the gear and supplies; she furnishes complete descriptions. Details about their clothing, contents of the "grub box"—what food items, utensils, etc. it contained—were all vivid in her memories. Also, how the wagon train was organized, how the livestock was trailed, and how the daily routine was kept on schedule; were all carefully assigned to a place in her memory.

Many adventures occurred on the route west: Enduring the dust and the heat, fording deep and swift rivers, plagues of mosquitoes and Mormon crickets, worries about hostile Indians, and then finally the rugged assent across the Blue Mountains, "all worse than your wildest imagination can fancy!"

In Utah these pioneers had traded their horses for oxen. Oxen promised to be stronger and more dependable in the rugged mountains ahead. Oxen were also less of a temptation to the Indians, who at this time were especially eager to steal horses to use in their raiding and warfare. Like milestones on their journey, they came to way stations and forts—Cheyenne, Ogden, Boise and Walla Walla. These locations had garrisons of soldiers for protection from Indians who had become increasingly hostile to the streams of immigrants.

Finally at Walla Walla they found an active little settlement where they could rest and restock supplies. Then they headed on north on the final leg of their journey. At the Snake River they crossed near Central Ferry. The Palouse River and Colfax were next. Then it was on to Hangman Creek where "Uncle Dick" Wimpy had homesteaded. At last in October of 1876 they arrived at their destination: "a new country with fresh challenges before us and a joy in our hearts that surpassed the strains and weariness of the long journey."

After a few days of rest along the stream the families moved their camp to the nearby foothills and cut logs for the buildings that would shelter them from the oncoming winter. After sufficient logs were skidded to the new home sites, everyone joined together to help with the house raisings in this new land.

Richard Wimpy was already established and was raising a large garden and a little grain. Livestock was his primary focus. He had secured a sizable herd of cattle. In cold weather he would butcher cattle and haul the meat to Walla Walla where he would then buy staples such as salt, sugar, kerosene and cloth. Hogs were another pioneer mainstay; they were primarily butchered and cured for home consumption. Wild meat was an important item, with venison and prairie chicken being plentiful. Amanda remembered the prairie chickens were so thick that her father killed four or five with one blast from a shotgun as the birds sat atop a little hay stack. Although Amanda does not mention them specifically, salmon would have been plentiful in their seasonal runs in Hangman Creek.

Amanda and her family's first Christmas in Washington Territory was a happy occasion. Family and neighbors were invited. Some, like the Spangles, far to the west, came almost twenty miles. Amanda related, "that all the good food, especially the pies," attested to the cooking ability of the pioneer wives. They provided a grand feast in this primitive setting.

In the evening the younger people had "a great time" dancing square dances and waltzes. The square dances were called by one of the Spangle boys while his brother played a violin. Someone with a French Harp also added to the music. The primitive frontier life made family and friends important and the desire to gather together to socialize and have a rare good time were given a special priority.

Amanda attended her first term of school in the winter of 1876-77. Richard Wimpy's daughter Belle taught five students, her four brothers and her cousin Amanda. Belle Wimpy had a rare qualification for her teaching chores. She alone, of her family, had briefly attended a mission school at Walla Walla. Amanda studied from two books, an old "blue speller" and a first grade reader. All writing and computations were done on slates. The first schoolroom was a bedroom in the Wimpy house.

The next year a primitive schoolhouse was built in the little settlement. It was a "box house" construction, rough, unpainted boards with "battens over the cracks." There were now eleven students for that second term. When the school term started in the fall most of the building was still unfinished and without the battens to cover the laps where the upright boards joined. Rough board benches for the students and a board table for the teacher made up the furnishings. Since the school had no clocks the teacher brought her own clock from home. As the sun shone through the cracks, she marked the movement of the sun's shadow along the wall to show the time. Then the clock could go back to the teacher's house and the marks would serve to tell the time. As winter approached, battens were added to the walls and a rough "box stove" was installed. Whether a school clock was then acquired was not addressed!

There were times of stark fear on the frontier. When the Nez Perce war started in 1877 there was a great concern that the local Coeur d'Alene Indians would join the uprising. Coeur d'Alene trails passed right by and Indian warriors frequently were seen. One night riders could be heard in the distance heading closer! Amanda's father quickly took his weapons and ammunition and told his family to seek cover in a partially dug well. Their relief was dramatic when they saw the riders were soldiers from a fort on the Spokane River. They were riding south to the Lewiston region to reinforce that meager garrison. Amanda never forgot how impressive the soldiers looked that night as their swords and bayonets caught the moonlight with a "brilliant and a breathtaking glitter!"

After a long summer of Indian scares, the Nez Perce hostiles were subdued and banished to Oklahoma. Still the fear of the Indians was near the surface for some time to come. Many of the families had stories of Indians coming by while the men folk were in the fields or away from home. These incidents almost always resulted in a sigh of relief when the Indians rode away and brought a silent "Thank you to the Almighty, that our time had not come!"

That same fall of 1877, a large contingent of Amanda's mother's family, the Andersons, came to the region with a group of fifteen wagons bringing new settlers. At that point the Andersons and the Wimpys made up the largest family group in the whole area.

Amanda Wimpy was born February 5, 1869 at Bentonville, Arkansas. While living near Latah she married Ephraim Nelson. They shortly moved to the Nez Perce Prairie when that area opened to homesteading. Later they moved to Clarkston. It was there, at the behest of her many descendants, she authored her story. Her comment to her family upon completing this project was, "read the story, enjoy it, and cherish the memory of those courageous ancestors who pioneered this great land of ours!"

Amanda lived until 1973, well into her 104th year.

Heartbreak And Pathos Could Be Part Of The Pioneer Experience

Of all the epic stories about the western migration to reach the northwestern frontier; and of all the tales that have recounted the hardship and the heartache that this historic trek could involve, none can surpass the story of Emeline Fuller and her family.

Their wagon train, containing approximately fifty people was attacked by Indians in the Snake River region of southern Idaho. This was in early September of 1860. The majority of these pioneers were killed or starved to death (29). Twelve survivors were eventually found by the army and taken to Fort Walla Walla. Several children taken captive were rescued the next year.

Emeline's story is part of a small book published by the Ye Galleon Press in 1992. This book also contains detailed research of army records concerning the massacre and rescue efforts by Spokane historian Carl Schlicke. A final element of local interest is the information in the introduction by local historian Glen Adams. This information relates that Emeline eventually married John Whitman and they were among the very earliest settlers at Rosalia, Washington. Later she also is reported to have married Andrew J. Calhoun, another early Rosalia area pioneer.

In her later years Emeline was prevailed upon by friends to put down the story of her life, particularly the horrific account of the wagon train massacre and the suffering and hardship that event entailed.

Emeline Trimble was born in 1847 at Mercellan, Wisconsin. She was the eldest of her parents' three children. In 1852 her father died of typhoid fever; then they lived with family members until her mother married a widower with six children. The next year a baby daughter arrived so at that point they made a family of twelve people.

Deliberating the prospects of a new life on the western frontier, they began to plan a trip to a new home and new opportunities in the Oregon country. On May 1 of 1860 they left on this great adventure, an adventure that began with the sorrow of leaving friends and familiar surroundings for an unknown future, a future which, in this case, was to have unbelievably dire consequences.

In its earlier stages, their wagon journey was very much like the typical trek. At first the travelers were in a large caravan with families heading for both California and the Oregon country. By the time they reached southern Idaho the number of immigrants was reduced by more than half. At that point, rising Indian hostility made it unsafe to proceed without the company of soldiers for protection.

The available soldiers were spread thin guarding the numerous wagon trains. Also, Emeline remembered that the commanding officer at Fort Hall, Idaho, was displeased about some aspect of their wagon train and sent along only a token force of a few soldiers. This was to be a tragic mistake! These small wagon caravans were the prime targets of the hostile Indians.

They traveled on with increasing Indian sightings and increasing evidence of Indian depredations against previous travelers. They were harried by brazen Indians who would want to trade or sell food for extravagant prices, and there was always a danger that the Indians would try to steal horses and cattle. At one place a previous train had buried a traveler. The Indians had dug up the body and had stolen the clothes. Then they reburied the body, leaving one hand and foot uncovered. This was to be an especially bad omen.

At this point the caravan had nine wagons. Sixteen men and boys were under arms. There were five women and twenty-one children between the ages of one and fourteen years. There were three soldiers and one "deserter" they picked up who had deemed it prudent to seek company in the wilderness. When the Indian attack became imminent, the soldiers spurred their horses to a full flight and left the settlers to their fate.

The Indians fell upon the group in a full frenzy. Rifle fire made any escape seem impossible as the victims fell and death was everywhere. Somehow Emeline took her baby sister into her arms, gathered her other siblings around her and told them they had to flee for their lives. A few other individuals from the group also fled the carnage. They escaped to the cover of willow trees along the nearby river.

From the little distance they could travel by nightfall, they saw the fires from the burning wagons. Then began a hide and seek nightmare of hiding by day and distancing themselves from the Indians by night. For several days they could occasionally see Indians in the distance and they assumed that they were trying to track them. After four days they saw nothing more to alarm them and they began to travel by day. They were a small group of less than a dozen survivors.

Reflect, if you will, Emeline was now barely thirteen years of age. She was a slender, slightly built child. Taking a nursing baby and four younger children, having only the clothes they were wearing and without provisions, into a barren wilderness. It was now the 10th day of September. Fall was in the air and the nights were turning cold.

What did they eat? After three days they killed their faithful family dog. Next was the only other surviving dog. Somewhat further along the river they came upon a gaunt cow that had somehow survived. The first shot fired since leaving the massacre site sealed her fate. The survivors roasted her and carried away with them what was left. They now estimated they had traveled about 100 miles.

So far all were alive but the suffering from hunger and exposure was intense. Without adequate clothes they suffered bitterly from the cold at night. More and more the survivors were like a small band of the "lost and the dammed" as they struggled slowly toward distant Fort Walla Walla.

Survival now became the overriding instinct. In Emeline's words, "Starvation was making sad inroads on the little band. None but those who endured the awful pangs of starvation can even have a faint idea of such suffering and death. We were frantic! Food we must have, but how could we get it? Then an idea took possession of our minds which at first we could not even mention to each other, so revolting to even think of, but the awful madness of hunger was upon us. We cooked and ate the bodies of the group members who had died. First to succumb were the littlest children."

In her account, Emeline goes into a detailed explanation of how she carried her baby sister in her arms and protectingly gave her every morsel of food she could. But it was of no avail. Emeline had carried her baby sister forty days. "I had to give her up and I was left alone," was her wrenching plaint.

By this stage forward progress of the party had stopped. One or two of the adults died and were buried; only to be later exhumed and used for sustenance.

Finally, piecemeal news of the wagon train disasters had reached Fort Walla Walla. Soldiers were dispatched to the region and they eventually reached the Owyhee River region and found the carnage of the massacre site. Just a little later they located the pitiful, starving survivors and the worst of the nightmare experience was over.

Emeline remembered the rescue scene and that she was too weak to have any real sensation of joy when she first saw the soldiers. Neither did she have much of an appetite. At first she could only eat part of a biscuit given to her by one of the officers. She went on to say, " I shall never forget the pitying looks bent on me by these strong men—tears stood in every eye."

There was still to be a long hard trek through snow and rough terrain across the Blue Mountains. Most of the survivors were so weak and infirm that they had to be carried in "hampers" and litters. By the last stage of the trip the people at Fort Walla Walla had heard of the rescue and the dire straits of the survivors. They sent wagons to meet them on the trail and additional food and clothing.

After a period of recuperation at the fort, Emeline went on to the Willamette Valley. Here she had an uncle and there were other settlers who had known her family. Life in Oregon was good, but Emeline's story states, "The sights of nature around me were charming to behold, but I could not help but turn my longing heart to my missing family and weep in loneliness. I would pray for my dear mother to come and take me, and cry myself to sleep."

Emeline had life long physical afflictions from her ordeal. Her feet were seriously injured from the effects of the flight after the massacre, "having no shoes and the bitter cold." Frequently she could not walk to school and required a horse for transportation. All of her life she was to repeat, "I still suffer much pain in my feet."

In November of 1863, Emeline married John M. Whitman. After a number of years the damp weather was difficult for Emeline's poor health and various physical problems. The Whitmans decided to move to a drier area in Washington Territory. Acquiring property at Rosalia, they kept a store-post office and a stage coach station.

The couple had a good life at Rosalia. Whitman became a successful busi-

Early Rosalia picture - from "Rosalia Community History"

nessman and community leader. He was also a major backer of efforts to get the first railroad service in the area to come through the town. He was to have a prominent part in the celebration to note the arrival of the first train. He was even to ride a handcar out to meet the train and be a special passenger as it chugged into town. Details of what happened vary somewhat in the retelling, but the most common version is that the engine hit the handcar and Whitman was killed!

Emaline and J.M. Whitman had only one child—a son who had died at nine years of age. Now Emaline was left alone and widowed. Major heartache had come again into her life.

Emaline returned to Wisconsin. Here she married again—a widower with seven children. This marriage was marked with family friction and they separated after only four years. It was at this point that family and friends requested she set down an account of her life and her "suffering by the Indians." This original account was published in 1892.

About 1900 she returned to Rosalia for a visit. In a dramatic quote she stated, "There is now a thriving town on my old place." Here Emaline married another prominent pioneer named Andrew J. Calhoun. They soon returned to Wisconsin. There were some reports that Calhoun died there in about 1909. When Glen Adams of the Ye Galleon Press reprinted Emaline's story in 1992 he tried to trace details of Emaline's death and burial. He was only able to report, "Here we lost all track of her." This seems to be a somewhat inauspicious ending to such a remarkable life and story!

A Footnote on the Andrew J. Calhoun Puzzle

The Calhouns were a large and an important pioneer clan in the Rosalia area. They had the common but confusing practice of carrying given names through several successive generations. The first local A.J. Calhoun came to the area in 1876 and settled near Spring Valley about five miles northeast of Rosalia.

A.J. Calhoun, Sr. had a very special distinction in area history. He is one of the first settlers credited with the foresight and ingenuity to demonstrate that the steep Palouse hills could raise good grain crops. At first, farming was only conducted on the flatter valleys and lowlands. Here because of production limitations and frost damage, grain farming was first believed to be only a marginal activity at best. This Calhoun also went on to achieve a notable place in local real estate and banking activities.

The senior Calhoun had five children including a boy called A.J., Jr. He grew up and took over the Spring Valley farm. The editor personally remembered him, about seventy years ago. He was an impressive looking elder with a long white beard and he was considered to be one of the oldest survivors of the pioneer era. It was easy for some of us local history enthusiasts to believe he was in the right time frame to be the senior Calhoun who was instrumental in the rise of grain farming and also to have been married to Emaline Fuller.

It also was easy to question whether Glen Adams was correct in his comments about the timing of the Calhoun-Fuller relationship, and Calhoun's death and burial in Wisconsin. Adams did not seem to be aware of the A.J., Sr. and A.J., Jr. name confusion. These circumstances provided an interesting puzzle for local historians. Fortunately a careful review of Rosalia's primary community history book and a search of local cemetery records has set the current generation straight and also provides an excellent example of the usefulness of historical records.

Native Son Comes By Wagon Train In 1873

(The following information is based on an interview published in the Spokesman-Review in October of 1943.) "Tum" Morris came to the northern Palouse country as a boy. After several false starts in finding a home and farm, the family settled in the Fairfield area where Tum spent the rest of his life. He was a popular, well liked man and became widely known as a repository of stories and experiences from pioneer days. He became active in pioneer associations both locally and in Spokane County associations. These are some of the highlights of his story.

Family Came By Wagon Train

The Morris family came west by wagon train in 1863. They had six children at this point. The family arrived at Walla Walla where they settled for a time. Here Tum arrived on the scene in early winter. The family was living in a log cabin on the bank of an interestingly named river—the Tum Tum. Morris explained, "That's how I got my name!"

By 1873 the family decided to come to the "upper county" north of the Snake River. The family had accumulated a large herd of cattle and they needed to locate where there was more open range. Late in November (which seems a debatable time to move), they started their journey north with two covered wagons and the cattle. Sure enough, the weather turned bitter cold with blowing snow.

They passed only three cabins on the way north—one on the Touchet River where Prescott is now, the ferryman's cabin at the Snake River, and finally a place where two brothers had a small ranch near Rock Lake. "We camped wherever night overtook us, sometimes having no water except as we melted snow. All of the provisions were frozen through. The men had to clear away a space in the snow and melt water and warm the food. We slept in the wagons and none too warm at that!"

After two years in the Sprague-Rock Lake area, the parents decided that they wanted to resettle where there would be more people and the children could attend school. In the spring of 1877, they headed north toward the Latah area looking for a new home site. They selected a place in Rock Creek Valley just east of the present site of Fairfield. "We were the first settlers here, but in a short time another family came and selected a place nearby."

The Indian Panic

Morris had an interesting comment concerning the local Indians. "The women dug the camas and did all the work while the men rode around on their cayuses. One day a young brave came out arrayed in all his war paint. He boastfully told my brother they were going on the war path and we would have to leave."

"Sure enough, we just got our garden planted when word came that the Nez Perce Indians had commenced trouble." The family quickly headed for Latah where the locals were gathering for protection. Then they received word that the soldiers had the situation controlled. This was just the start of rumors and panic that came at intervals all through the summer. Tum's father and brothers had planned to return to Walla Walla anyway to work in the grain harvest and they continued on that course.

When the family finally returned that fall they had a very rude surprise! They found their new neighbors had jumped their claim and were holding it for themselves. Fortunately, Major Richard Wimpy, a prominent pioneer and the Hangman area's first settler, told them about an area just west of Fairfield. It was a valley called Rattler's Run.

"This name would naturally cause one to think of snakes, but that was not the case. The name was given because a famous dog named Rattler used to chase deer and coyotes up and down the creek." "Coming to this place, my folks liked it the best of any place they had seen, and being the first to come they had a free choice to settle wherever they wanted in that little valley."

At once they proceeded to build a cabin and kept busy splitting rails to fence their land. That little cabin stood as a landmark in that area for about sixty-five years.

In the summer of 1878, there were again alarming reports of Indian trouble. This time the stories were that the Umatilla Indians had gone on the warpath.

"This time we decided not to run, but with the aid of other settlers, built a stockade on the place adjoining ours. We did this by erecting two long log buildings; then dug a trench and set a double row of logs, 12 to 15 feet high, around them. Portholes were cut through these logs. This was built around a spring to insure a water supply. When completed, it was stocked with provisions and those who lived farthest away moved in."

"Only a few of these settlers had firearms, so I was sent to get signers to a petition asking the government to furnish guns. I'll confess this trip took all the courage I had, for as I rode along I imagined I could see Indians behind every stump and tree. But all this preparation was unnecessary, for in a short time we were delighted to hear that the soldiers had the Indians under control. Since then, there has never been any serious trouble with the Indians in this area."

Tum Morris had a final heart-wrenching story of pioneer life. "The fall of 1879 brought a sad trial to our family when all of the six children had diphtheria. My sister, eleven, lived but a few days and the second day after this, two brothers passed away. At this time I was unconscious and they thought every hour would be my last. There was no doctor within reach and we had no medicine. It is difficult to realize the anxiety and helpless feeling any one would have under such circumstances. Our only assistance was two or three bachelors who had heard of our trouble and came to offer help. The bodies were temporarily buried on the home-place, but were removed to Mount Hope when the cemetery was started there." These are just a few of the events that make up the pioneer saga of

Tum Morris.

> *There is one other interesting regional story concerning the "Rattler's Run" stream and valley and a Tum Morris relative. This is from a local newspaper account of March 1910 (Fairfield Standard):*
>
> *"Miss Grace Darknell narrowly escaped drowning Tuesday noon, in Rattler's Run, about 1 1/2 miles north of Fairfield.*
> *Miss Darknell was on her way home from town, driving a single horse top buggy. Finding the water had risen and was running around the first bridge north of the Doepke place (near present day Highway 27) she attempted to drive through, thinking she could keep in the road and reach the bridge without difficulty. The horse struck the corner of the bridge on the upper side and at once the buggy tipped over throwing Miss Darknell into the stream which here had a current like a mill-race. She was carried under or over three bridges and went through or over three barbed wire fences before she was rescued by Charles Leoffler (Loeffler) at a point about a quarter of a mile below the bridge. During part of the time she was conscious though she does not remember much about her thrilling watery trip. She made an effort to keep her lungs inflated, to float face upwards and to avoid swallowing the muddy water. This presence of mind probably saved her. The swiftness of the current was also in her favor, but the whole affair seems almost miraculous. She was unconscious and chilled so that some difficulty was experienced in restoring the normal warmth to her body. At latest reports she was doing well and it is not thought that any serious results will follow her long immersion in ice cold water. The horse was drowned, probably before it got loose from the buggy and was found in a shallow cove a few rods below the bridge..."*

The Alice Lederer Story

Alice Mooney Lederer lived to become one of the last links with the pioneer era in the northern Palouse. She was a descendant of "Wagon Train" ancestors. The span of time she lived through was an era of immense change. It reached from the frontier to the age of modern technology.

Alice was an avid witness of this period. Her keen observations and memories provide a remarkable record of our area's history and events. She relates the following details:

My grandparents (Andersons) lived in Carthage, Missouri. They and their families endured real hardships and heartbreaks in the Civil War era. This was a "border" area where divided sympathies created chaos. Looting, burning of homes, and even killings were part of their regular existence. During the war, one of the family's sons slipped home to see his family. So-called "bushwhackers" caught him and told him to run for his life. They shot him in the back and killed him! Even after the war, guerrilla forces kept the area in turmoil.

Final discomforting factors were that this same area was plagued by serious health problems. Malaria, then known as ague or night fever, was a common and debilitating disease. This in the same way as the Wimpys' seemed more than ample reason to seek a new start in the distant northwest.

In 1877 they set out on the six-month trip from Carthage to Walla Walla. There were a hundred wagons in the caravan. Alice Lederer's grandfather was chosen to be the captain of the train. These pioneers had a full range of the typical experiences of this epic journey. Dust and heat, fording swift rivers, Indian scares, births of babies, deaths of the sick and the weak, tedious and rugged daily routines; these were all hallmarks of the journey.

At one camping place along the Snake River they found a site where people from an earlier wagon train had evidently been massacred by Indians. There were human skull bones, broken dishes and parts of wagons. "The men did not go to bed that night and the women didn't sleep," was the somber journal entry.

Crossing the Rockies was a rugged ordeal. They often thought the wagons would tip over or shake to pieces. At Walla Walla they rested for a week, bought some supplies and headed further north into Washington Territory. Around the first of October they arrived at their "promised land" near present day Latah.

Alice had her own comments about Major Richard H. Wimpy, who had come to this region from Missouri in 1872, was there to greet the new arrivals. It was he who had been influential in getting the Andersons and other Wimpys to choose this destination. At this point they were easily one of the largest family groups in the northern Palouse. When Major Wimpy and his family first came in 1872, they carried a cookstove and all of their other possessions on pack horses from Walla Walla. They also brought a sizable number of cattle and that was their primary livelihood. Wimpy homesteaded 160 acres and took up another 160-acre timber culture claim.

The later coming settlers also filed on 160-acre homesteads, built cabins and barns and "began the typical pioneer life." Alice further commented, "They plowed soil that had never been turned before. Indians had lived here for thousands of years, but it was the first time the earth had been plowed."

Wimpy was raising an extensive garden by the time the others arrived and he was able to help supply food while the latecomers were getting established. He had also begun raising grain and in that regard he is mentioned in a number of accounts as the source of seed for many of the first farming efforts.

These comments are followed with stories about the Indian scares of 1877 when the Nez Perce uprising occurred. "Lots of people were driven from their homes by fears of the hostile Indians." Many local people gathered together and "forted up" in stockades or defensible places. Some fled as far as Walla Walla where larger numbers of white people afforded protection. At Spokane Falls, settlers took refuge on Havermale Island. Local army troops tried to protect the region, but they were spread extremely thin over the vast area.

When Indian hostilities ended, frontier life returned to normal and life went on. Alice's mother and sister married George Huffman and Cornelius Mooney in a double wedding at Farmington. The ceremony was performed while the two couples sat in a horse-drawn hack. The minister was known as "Preacher Wright."

Alice remembered this special story about the minister. He had a small garden in Farmington and it was hard to get good quality garden seed. Someone gave him a little choice seed corn, just enough for one row. He was dropping it ever so carefully in the row when he came to the end of the row and looked around. One of his chickens had followed behind him and eaten it all. This would never do! He caught and killed her, got back his seed corn, planted it again, "and all was well."

Not much later the couple took a stagecoach trip from Farmington to Lewiston. One of Mooney's friends, Felix Warren, who later was to achieve widespread fame as a teamster—he once drove a forty-horse span at a Chicago World's Fair—drove the coach. The Lewiston Hill road was little more than a trail in those days. It was a steeper, shorter route than today. The driver whipped up his horses as fast as they could go all the way down. Meanwhile, he was yelling as loud as he could for anyone who might be coming to get out of the way. They skidded to a stop at the ferry and crossed the river to the only hotel—all in only 30 minutes. Needless to say, the couple was thoroughly frightened and Mrs. Mooney stated adamantly, "she would rather have walked down!"

One of Mrs. Lederer's uncles at Latah was quite a hunter. He had a pack of hounds to hunt coyotes, bear, bobcats and lynx. Sometimes he also trapped animals and on occasion would bring in an animal he had caught to display to the locals. One day he drove into town with his wagon loaded with a big high box covered with canvas and wire netting over the top. He put his two sons on either side for "guards." Then he drove down the main street of Latah calling to everyone to come and see the lynx he had caught. When a crowd had gathered, he threw back the canvas and there for all to see were two links of chain! Did we say he was also quite a bit of a cut up and a trickster?

Alice had another story she enjoyed telling. As a girl, she had two close friends with whom she enjoyed many adventures. They decided to make a horseback trip to Spokane Falls. North of Spangle, two Indians rode out of the timber and chased the girls. They were very frightened and rode their poor horses hard to get away. She later decided the Indians were probably just trying to scare them. She added, "If so, they certainly succeeded!"

Some of Alice's other popular stories were the experiences of her father, Cornelius Mooney, when he was one of the first horseback mail riders in the north Palouse. He was a new arrival in the area when he heard there was a job available carrying mail from Lewiston to Pine Grove (today's Spangle).

On his first run with the mail, he had never been through this area and he felt very fortunate not to get lost as the country was very sparsely settled. There was only one bridge on the route (probably on the Palouse River). The rest of the streams had to be forded. There was a store and a post office at Farmington and a post office at Major Wimpy's on Hangman Creek. Again, Pine Grove (Spangle) was the final stop.

Mud was usually one of the worst hindrances. Many times he had to walk and lead his horse through the worst spots. He changed horses at about fifteen mile intervals. Hangman Creek was the worst obstacle because it had to be crossed several times. Near Latah there was a "foot pole" where he could cross on a log while the horse swam the creek. The bank was very steep here and once the horse and rider both went over backwards. Luckily, both landed safely.

Later the local people built a bridge across Hangman Creek between Tekoa and Latah. One cold spring morning when Mooney came to this spot, the bridge was gone! The ice breaking up had destroyed it. Just a short way back there was a house and the creek was still ice covered. Mooney called across to ask if he could borrow a horse if he walked across on the weak ice. The answer was affirmative, so he tethered his horse and walked across. On the return trip he was told the ice "went out" only about fifteen minutes after he had crossed!

Mooney was carrying the mail when the Nez Perce War broke out! The country was in turmoil with all sorts of wild rumors and alarms. There were at least two reports that Mooney had been killed by hostile Indians.

Mooney was a man who tried a wide variety of jobs and farming endeavors. All of these made a wide and interesting variety of experiences for his family, and his daughter Alice seemed to enjoy them all.

Note: It is rather common to speak of early-day mail riders as the "Pony Express" mail. This term properly applies only to a short-lived mail system from St. Joseph, Missouri to Sacramento, California. It had relay stations about every twenty miles, between which small, wiry men rode fresh horses at breakneck speed halfway across the continent. Regular pioneer mail was hardly ever "express" delivery.

Alice Mooney Lederer lived to almost her 102nd birthday. She was widely known and appreciated as one of the last survivors of a remarkable period of history in the northern Palouse.

CHAPTER 4

The Wild West

Vigilantes Ride In Rock Creek Valley

Time was in this region when it was a real struggle to establish law and order. The frontier was frequently poorly served by the law. Sheriffs and law officers were few and far between and the "criminal element" was plentiful, drawn by the free and easy atmosphere of the new land. People could frequently be frustrated by this situation, and, from this frustration, they might take the law into their own hands; sometimes with wrenching results.

Some classic stories and folklore evolved from these conditions and some of them seem never to have gotten old in the retelling. A classic example is the story of the lynching of Aldy Neil.

The Lynching of Aldy Neil

Much of this story traces to the research done by area resident Herb Stevens over fifty years ago. For a considerable part of his life he lived in the Fairfield-Rockford area. Stevens tried to reconstruct events surrounding this 1882 incident by talking to area old-timers. By then they were some sixty years later in time. Memories had dimmed and many details were hear-say—often disputed and controversial. Stevens wrote up what he was able to find about the lynching in a small book that was published by the Ye Galleon Press in Fairfield. It was titled: Vigilantes Ride in 1882.

Some Background

The Stevens' account begins with some descriptions of the location, and the beauty and fertility of the Rock Creek Valley area east of Fairfield and Rockford. This made it a magnet for settlement in the 1870's. On the south fork of Rock Creek a large group of settlers came into the area from the Willamette Valley in Oregon. Many of them had been friends or neighbors and they also had a common religious affiliation. When they settled they soon built the Rock Creek Bethel Methodist Church—one of the first Methodist churches north of the Snake River. Aldy Neal's family was part of this group.

About this time, rustling was pervasive throughout much of the Inland Northwest. From eastern Oregon and the Walla Walla region stolen livestock—particularly horses—were driven all the way to distant points like northern Idaho and western Montana. Even the minefields up in British Columbia provided a beckoning market.

It is not very well remembered today how much of a movement of people and goods accompanied the mining booms of this era. Mining was the engine that really drove the area economy. Agriculture was pretty minimal at this point—especially farming. But the demand for livestock, especially horses, found a ready market at the mine fields. One of the main routes for the movement of animals came through Rock Creek Valley.

There were some intriguing aspects to the rustling trade. Horses stolen in the southern regions would be driven to the northern markets. This helped confuse their identity and ownership. In the same way, horses stolen in the north would be driven back to the south and resold. It was an ideal business plan—an unending inventory of merchandise and customers. The only drawback was that some people objected to the legal status of the whole affair!

The Story Continues

The next phase of this affair is somewhat akin to a soap opera story. Aldy, of course is the central character, but he is certainly a rather "cloudy" individual when it comes to any specific details. There are even disputes about the correct spelling of his name. Allie, Aldy or All-day are common variations.

There are disputes about his age. Some accounts say he was an "innocent boy" of nineteen—which was the common story for a long time. Later research gave his age as about thirty years old. This same research showed that he had several arrest convictions at Cheney. Cheney was the county seat at that point. Stolen livestock was involved in these charges. That pretty well blows the story of an innocent nineteen year old.

Then there are disputes about Aldy's family relationships. Some accounts say he was an orphan. Other accounts mention his father being in the area when Aldy died. His father's brother was nicknamed "Red" and is always said to have been an evil character. In 1882 Aldy was watching stock for him in the valley.

Finally, there are questions about whether Aldy was a little slow mentally—making him an easy target for a scapegoat in this whole sordid mess. As a psychologist would say today, many of the individuals in this story were a "little dysfunctional."

In June of 1882 several local horses disappeared. This was the straw that broke the camel's back! The following Sunday after church service there was a meeting to plan a course of action. "Red" was the prime suspect and it would seem his doom was sealed. A contingent of locals went to confront Red, but he glibly pointed the blame at Aldy and somehow diverted the group from himself.

Aldy was only a mile or so away. When he saw the men bearing down on him he knew there was trouble brewing. He barricaded himself in his cabin, ready for a standoff. After some palaver through the cabin door, Aldy was promised safe conduct to Cheney to face charges—Aldy surrendered to this offer.

Aldy was then loaded on a buggy with three or four guards and they started out almost due north, heading for a main junction of Rock Creek. It is important to note that the county seat lay straight to the west, so this was a wide detour. As dark was falling on that long summer day they were intercepted by a lynch gang at the main creek fork. A bit of a sham fight was said to have occurred, but Aldy was quickly taken by the group and strung up from the branch of a nearby pine tree. There his body hung until the next day.

The sheriff at Cheney was called. He made a leisurely, low key appearance without any real action. At first any outcry about a miscarriage of justice was muted at best.

There was no formal cemetery at Rockford and Aldy is said to be buried on the hill north of town not far from Highway 27. Sometime later history minded people had a marker made. Today, no one seems to know the location of Aldy's grave or several other graves said to be on this hillside. At present, in editing this current account, I can find no one that can place the location of these graves and there is also a question of what ever happened to the marker?

Another Researcher Appears

An interesting aspect of this old story came along about fifteen years ago. A lady from Oregon by the name of Norma Eid came to this area, saying she was a distant relative of the Neil family. She had made a major study of family history and she was determined to do some serious research because she knew so much of the story was based on hearsay and details that she felt were untrue.

It was she who came forward with the information that Aldy was about thirty years old, that he was not an orphan and that much of what had been said about the Neil family and others involved was faulty. Ms. Eid was determined to do serious research and she had the background and know-how to research legal records and newspaper accounts of that long ago time. It was Eid who set the record straight about Aldy's previous arrests—she did not shy away from unpleasant facts.

She put together some interesting connections of Rock Creek Valley families, including the Neils, that had ties to Montana and elsewhere that placed them in contact with people involved in the rustling routes mentioned earlier. This reinforces the supposition that Aldy was a scapegoat to take attention from a number of other individuals.

A final interesting part of the Eid's research was the fact that the Rock Creek Valley hanging made major headlines in a surprising number of newspapers. The hanging was roundly decried over much of the Inland Northwest and the news accounts made it as far as Helena, Montana, to the east and to San Francisco on the west coast.

Another individual has some input to add to the Aldy Neil story. Glen Adams, area historian and publisher, took a deep interest in this historical event when he published the Herb Stevens' book. There had always been talk of the participation and involvement of local people in this sordid affair. Adams found one story in particular that was of great interest. A well known, respected man named Samuel F. Starr, "confessed" to an involvement. A public road in southern Spokane County carries the Starr family name. The most important landmark in that part of the valley is today called Starrs Butte.

Starr's, and at least one other "confession," were said to have appeared in local papers. Glen Adams verified the existence of these confessions through research that pointed him to stories in the Fairfield Standard newspaper of long ago.

Some Footnotes

An interesting addition to this story is the folklore that typically tells of the "punishment" that comes to participants in this sort of an event—namely gruesome and violent deaths. Stories about deaths in strange fires, gorings and tramplings by animals, violent accidents and strange illness—these were reputedly the fate of most lynch gang members. Finally the hanging tree is eventually always disfigured and scarred. Sure enough, lighting reportedly brought down the hanging tree east of Rockford!

Finally, Aldy's cap has a place in the ending of this story. The cap was apparently kicked aside during the struggle at the lynching. A day or two later an elderly Coeur d'Alene Indian woman came walking into Rockford. Perched on her head was the cap that some of the locals could identify as Aldy's. For a long time after, it was to be a part of her "going to town" apparel.

This would be just one more of the ironies that are so much a hallmark of this tale.

The Masterson Gang

In the decade that followed the Rock Creek Valley lynching there was a major build-up in livestock stealing a little farther south. By this time more people had moved into the Palouse and stock raising had a big expansion. In the Whitman County area ranchers had so much trouble with rustling that they formed the Stock Raisers Protective Association. Members put in money and the county would often add another $500.00 a year. In the early 1890's they hired special deputies and in general tried to put major pressure on the stock thieves. In a two-year period as many as twenty-five rustlers were apprehended.

Still these efforts met with only a partial success. The Endicott-LaCrosse area was a hot-bed of livestock thefts. Closer to the north Palouse, another hot spot was the "Hole in the Ground" area near Pine City. Stolen stock from a wide area was stashed in hiding in this isolated and desolate area. Rugged terrain and box canyons made this locale a real rustlers' stronghold.

At one point a special deputy successfully infiltrated the rustlers' gang and cased their hiding places. He relayed this information to the Stock Raisers Association and they mounted a large posse. A major gun battle and shootout took place and for quite a while the area was quiet as the rustlers scattered.

One of the dominant figures in the rustlers' ranks was a man named Billy Masterson. He was described as a big, athletic man and he was personable and a natural leader. But he also had a mean, gritty side and many people commented on the cold, steely look in his eyes.

Billy was said to be a close relative of "Bat" Masterson, the famed western lawman. Some accounts say they were brothers; other accounts suggest they were cousins. At any rate, they followed very different paths where the law was concerned.

Masterson's main sidekick and aid was his son-in-law, a man called Ed Harris. Masterson's daughter Mary also relished the excitement of this sort of a rough and lawless life. Even when the law was hot on the heels of her male family members, she rode by their side.

In 1891 when rustling was at a high pitch it was causing a major concern among the stockmen. Accordingly the "heat was on" in all quarters of the northwest. So when the Colfax sheriff received a wire from Montana telling that they had apprehended Ed Harris there, he took immediate action. He quickly wired back to hold him until deputies could be sent to pick him up. These lawmen made a quick trip to Montana by rail and returned to Spokane with Harris in custody. Here they had to lay over to wait for a train to Colfax.

Masterson had heard of Harris' arrest and was keeping an eye on the train from Montana. He had an "associate" with him for back up help. When Harris was being held over in a hotel, Masterson somehow wrangled permission to speak with "his beloved daughter's husband." This made up a group of three deputies, Masterson and his friend, and Harris at the hotel.

One deputy left briefly to attend to some business. Then one of the remaining deputies needed to visit the "washroom." Masterson saw his chance, turned off the light, drew his weapon and fired at the deputy point-blank. But the deputy thought as quickly as Masterson. Cat-like, he leaped aside and fired back point-blank. When the light was turned back on, the notorious Bill Masterson lay dying. Three bullets—one just over his heart—had done him in! Immediately the melee was over. Masterson's friend made a quick get-away. This event received wide coverage in all the Spokane and area newspapers.

Harris was quickly taken to Colfax where he was put on trial. He was found guilty and sentenced to a long term in the penitentiary at Walla Walla.

> *Note: Harris was not to stay behind bars very long. He hid himself in a load of prison made bricks being hauled into Walla Walla and escaped. Not too surprisingly, Ed and Mary Harris were reportedly never to be seen again.*

Vigilante 'Justice' In Whitman County

Whitman County might rank high if there was ever a competition for vigilante hangings. It has never exactly been a subject for bragging rights—it certainly does not suit the majority of people's sense of justice. However in times past there was often a sizable group of people who agreed that desperate deeds and times called for desperate measures, especially when law enforcement was perceived as weak or lacking. Still, when the law was pushed aside and mob action took over, it was almost always roundly condemned—after the deed was done.

In the last fifteen years of the 1800's, insult was added to injury when a surprising number of prisoners put in the jail in the courthouse at Colfax were broken out of their jail cells by "vigilante gangs" and hanged on site.

The first of the courthouse lynchings was in 1884. Louis Knott was accused of murdering William Higgins of Pullman. There was a wide dissatisfaction with the settlement of the case. While Knott was being held in jail the sheriff was tricked out of his house near the courthouse on a false pretense and he was forced to give up the jail keys. Then the jail guard was also threatened and pushed aside.

Knott was taken out into the jail yard and backed up against the jail yard fence. Here a rope was tossed over a fence post to perpetrate the grisly hanging.

Ten years later two men both received similar treatment. Their names were George Parker and Ed Hill. Both men had some previous scrapes with the law, but the homicides they each were charged with were based largely on circumstantial evidence. Ed Hill in particular had received a light sentence. His trial had been moved to neutral ground at Dayton. After the trial the comment was made, "The light sentence will do him little good if you ever take him back to Colfax." Within two weeks the lynchings occurred.

The lynching gang formed specifically to zero in on Parker's punishment. Hill was immediately also apprehensive. Sure enough the gang forced its way into his cell as well. He swore he was not the man responsible for the homicide, but his fate was sealed.

The courthouse jail was on the second floor. One after another both men were hung from the windows over the main entrance. There was to be no doubt about the meaning of this example.

Some historians say that while Whitman County had invested the time and money needed to perform legal executions, none had yet been carried out by 1898. In January of 1898 another lynch mob kept that record intact.

Charles (alias Blackie) Marshall and Robert (alias Dakota Slim) McDonald were arrested for the alleged murder of Orville Hayden. Both men were transients. "Blackie" had one other major handicap in the areas of potential fair treatment—he was a Negro.

The crime occurred in Farmington in a bar. For the record the bar was just east of town and actually across the Idaho line. Probably drinking laws were involved. Hayden was from a well known local family. This probably helped prejudice the case. Anyway both were charged and brought to trial at Colfax.

Legal issues created a lot of wrangling by the judge and the attorneys. The case dragged on and on. The delays were the basis for the mob action. When the lynch party organized they broke into the jail. They got Blackie out of his cell immediately, put a rope around his neck and hung him from a courthouse window.

Dakota Slim heard the commotion and correctly assumed he would be in for the same treatment. When the mob showed up at his cell he loudly pleaded for his life. He did more! He had stuffed the key hole to the cell door with paper. Slim was also brandishing a case knife he had wetted razor sharp. He had attached the knife to a mop stick and he kept ramming it through the cell door bars. All the while he kept yelling he was innocent of the murder. It had already been a long night and the mob fury had burned out enough that they gave up and left the building.

A local newspaper account said, "Once again a gruesome sight has defaced the temple of justice." And sure enough the rope mark on the window ledge verified the foul deed. Another quote was that, "It took the combined efforts of seven men to pull the corpse up through the window." The paper also described the men carrying the body to the closest undertaking parlor. "There it was viewed during the day by many hundreds of people."

Life on the frontier often hardened men and it seemed crime could be pervasive. The black stains of vigilante action can be explained, but it can never be excused or condoned.

Note: Elliot Gay's somewhat rare book titled, "Yesterday and the Day Before" provided parts of the information in the last two stories. It is an intriguing book, primarily focusing on Whitman County, but it also covers a wider range of pioneer lore. It is available in some of the region's library systems. It is to be recommended to history buffs.

A current reference map of the Northern Palouse

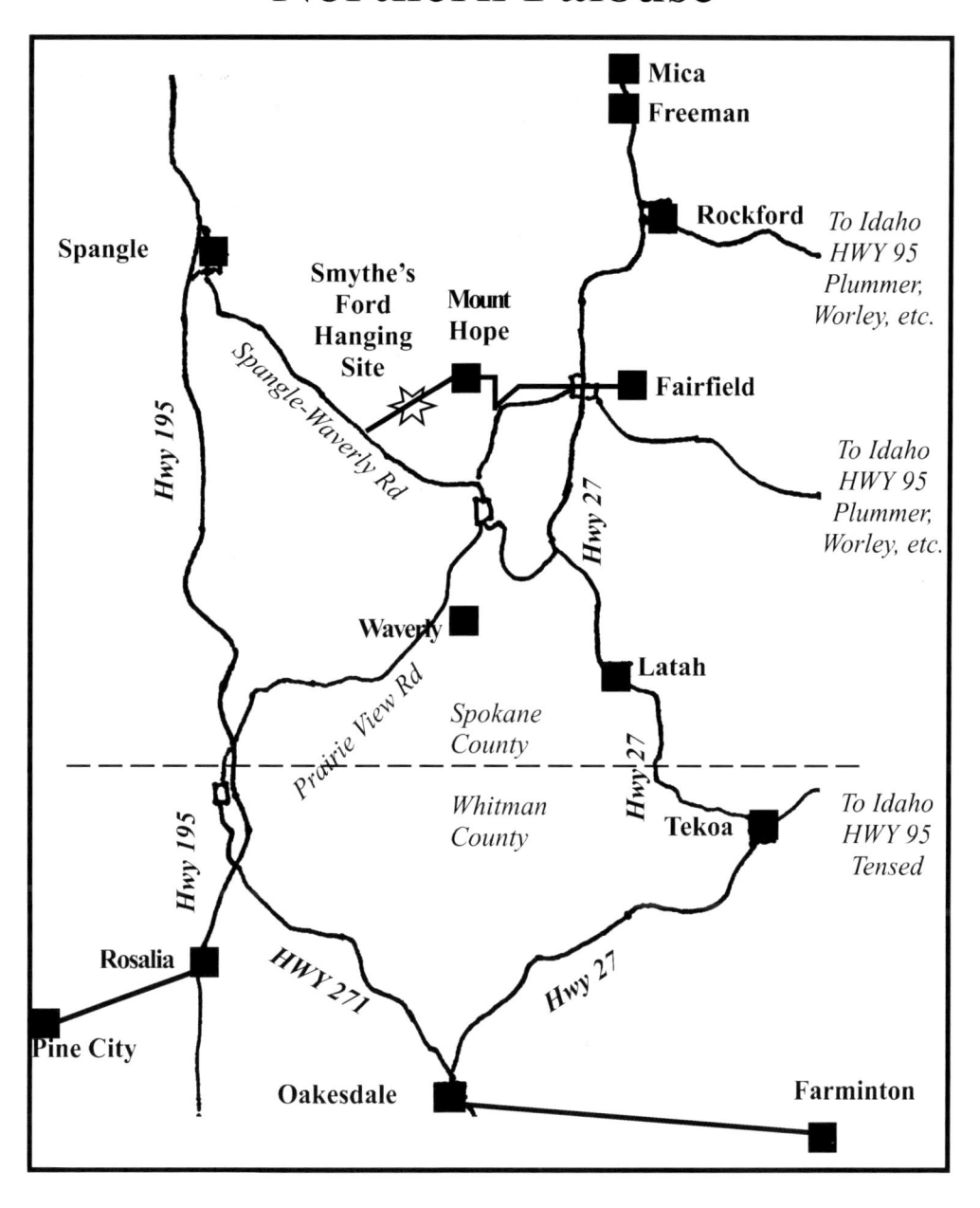

45

CHAPTER 5

Some Maps That Connect Area History

Maps as an Aid

Few tools will provide more assistance in gaining a grasp of local history than a study of old maps. The number and variety of these maps can be surprising. We will be able to consider just a few of them; and we should remember that different maps may have varying details and emphasis. Taken together, they comprise a wealth of information that will make history come alive in a very special way.

Land Survey Maps

A good starting place for our purposes is the original Palouse region survey maps of the 1870s. The surveys were made to lay out the townships, sections and quarter sections that would be needed for homesteading and proper acquisition of land, as settlement was beginning. It was clear that the area was on the cusp of a dramatic population influx.

In the process of mapping this region, the major reference points were the Willamette Meridian (range) and degrees north of the equator. Range and degrees together are basic and essential references. To illustrate it and other mapping techniques, we will look at a typical township in the north Palouse.

The 1873 Land Survey Map of Waverly Township. This township is identified and designated as township 21 N (north), R (range) 44 E (east). That identity locates it precisely in the vast reaches of the inland northwest.

An initial step in a township survey was to divide its 36 square miles and its 23,040 acres into precise smaller units. A township has 36 numbered sections. Each section contains 640 acres. The numbering began with Section 1 in the upper right corner of the map, then running left through Section 6. It then drops down directly below to Section 7 and then across to Section 12. It continues in a crisscross pattern to Section 36 at the lower right corner of the map.

Individual sections are further divided into 160-acre parcels (quarter sections). A location marker and survey point, usually a stone, is placed at the center of each section. Quarter sections can be divided further using the location marker as a reference, but the main initial purpose was to allow the identification of 160-acre homestead tracts and also to identify the land that was granted to the railroads for their construc-

1873 Land Survey Map of Waverly Township

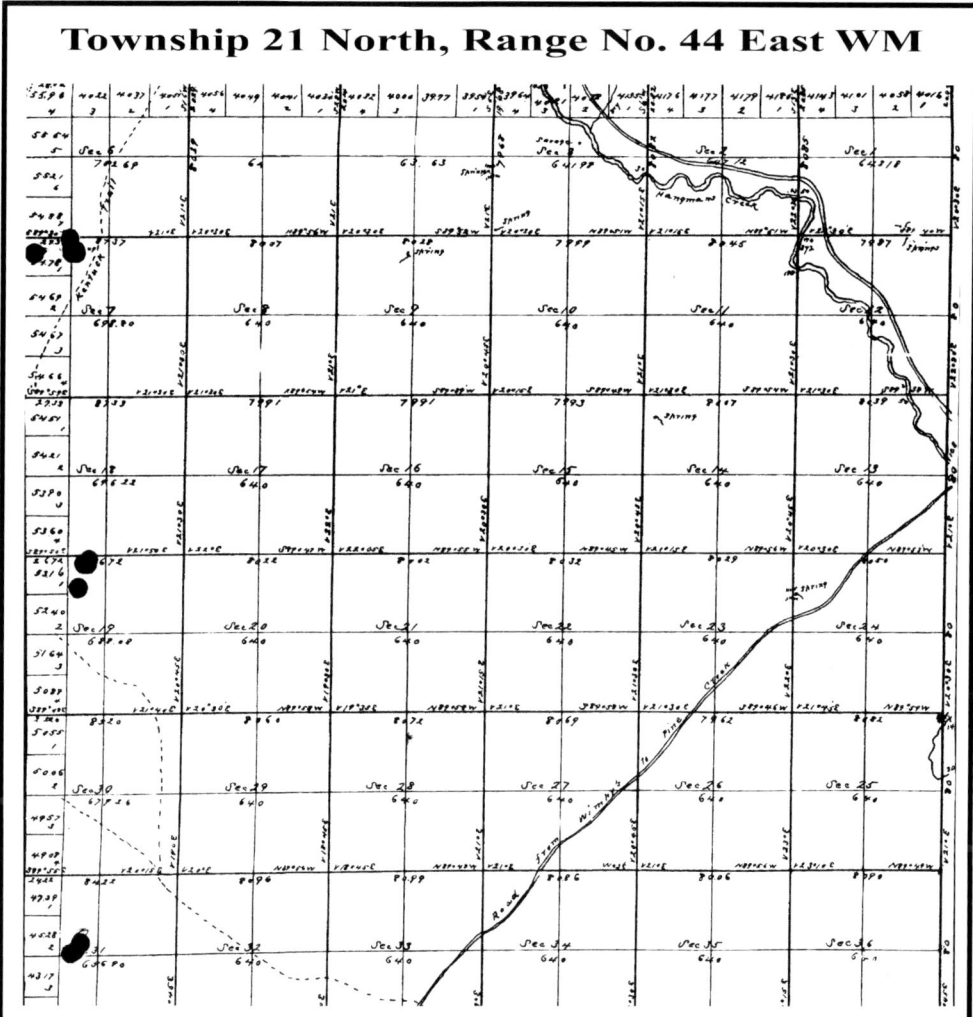

Township 21 North, Range No. 44 East WM

This 1873 Land Survey Map is from the U.S. Bureau of Land Management office at Spokane. These original surveys are on microfilm along with homestead applications. They are available for a nominal fee.

tion efforts.

Several other facts connect with these surveys. We should first note that there is a large amount of historic romance with the concept of a vast frontier open to homesteading. It is common to believe that most of the west was opened to settlement by filing a homestead claim and getting free possession of the land by the process of working and improving it. In fact, only the even-numbered sections were available for homesteading. In addition, sections 16 and 36 were always set aside as "state land" and were usually dedicated to the support of a school system. So actually, only 14 sections (less than half) were free homestead land, and the odd-numbered sections were granted to the railroads. This railroad property was almost always immediately put up for sale. Prices might range from about $2.50 per acre to $5.00 or more, based on location and quality of the soil.

Returning to the survey procedures, a survey crew consisting of a head surveyor and several assistants had a big job. It would usually take a month or more to establish the boundaries, lay out the sections and place the center markers.

The head surveyor would also write a full geographic description of the township. He would describe the topography, the vegetation and the physical features such as springs, creeks and trails. These reports are of great interest and answer the questions about what the country was like when the first white men came to settle in the area. The survey report would include an appraisal of the area's potential for future use. In this locale, the rolling dune-like hills, the fertile soil and the stirrup-high grass were the dominant features. A little ponderosa pine adjacent to Hangman Creek and the rosebush, service berry and other shrubs on the steep north slopes were also noted. The chief surveyor offered the outlook of a great potential for a livestock industry. He did not foresee the rise of grain farming which would be the real hallmark of this region.

With the hilly terrain and primitive survey procedures, a feature of the local township mapping required "correction units." These would be located on two sides of each township, and they compensated for local deviations and would hopefully make corrections before they would adversely affect the accuracy of larger scale maps.

Inaccuracies Still Did Occur

An interesting example of early survey problems was the discovery that the boundary between the Washington and Idaho Territories was flawed. When it was later re-surveyed, some post offices were in a different territory than had been supposed.

Today these old survey maps can be found at the Bureau of Land Management in Spokane where they are on microfilm. Another historical resource available here are the records of homestead applications, the applicant's name, date of filing and the date of the homestead grant five years later. Genealogists may find this information to be of special interest. Today family farms that originated with a homestead grant are becoming rare, and a homestead grant signed by a president of that period is a highly-priced document.

> *Spokane Bridge was located near today's Washington-Idaho border in the Spokane Valley. It was a transportation hub of a vast area, being on the Mullan Road and the northern terminus of the Kentuck Trail. A significant town grew up here with stores and hotels. Most significantly, it had the very first post office in this part of the inland northwest. This post office was first believed to be in Idaho Territory. It was corrected to properly be in Washington Territory, as a result of the later Boundary Survey. Today this site is near the Washington State Port of Entry on I-90. The town has long disappeared, and its early importance is not well remembered.*
>
> *Another example of survey error was the required correction of the west boundary of the Coeur d'Alene Indian Reservation. Chief Andrew Seltice (prominently mentioned elsewhere in this book) had settled on land just east of Tekoa where he had a large farm. When the boundary error was discovered, he had to move his home and farm operation a mile or more to the east to be on the reservation.*

It is interesting to note that a significant number of applicants did not hold and work their claims long enough to acquire title. If they ran out of energy and enthusiasm, they could sell their "right" for what the market would pay and walk away. The new operator could complete the terms of the contract and finish the transaction.

The hard work and primitive, lonely life of the frontier was not for everyone. But for the people from the crowded east and for countless thousands of emigrants, this was the way for them to achieve their part of the American Dream.

An Example of a Request for a Post Office

A copy of a rare request form and a sketch map can be found in one of the Rosalia area's early-day histories. This form and map provide information that is both interesting and of considerable historical significance. The author is not aware of the existence of any other of these applications in this region surviving.

The Rosalia area had a small handful of settlers who wanted mail service by 1872. This required a formal request form to be submitted, and this process was begun in the summer.

J. I. Favorite was filing the request for the post office to be in his home, and he was applying for the position of Postmaster. Rosalia was the requested name, because that was Favorite's wife's name. Their home was 2 1/2 miles north of the present town. It remained there until John M. Whitman became postmaster and moved the facility to the present town location where he had established a store and stagecoach depot.

Rosalia was then on the principal route from Colfax to Spokane Falls, on what was called the Territorial Road. This road was improved as a primary pioneer travel route in the early 1870s.

For map references see following page.

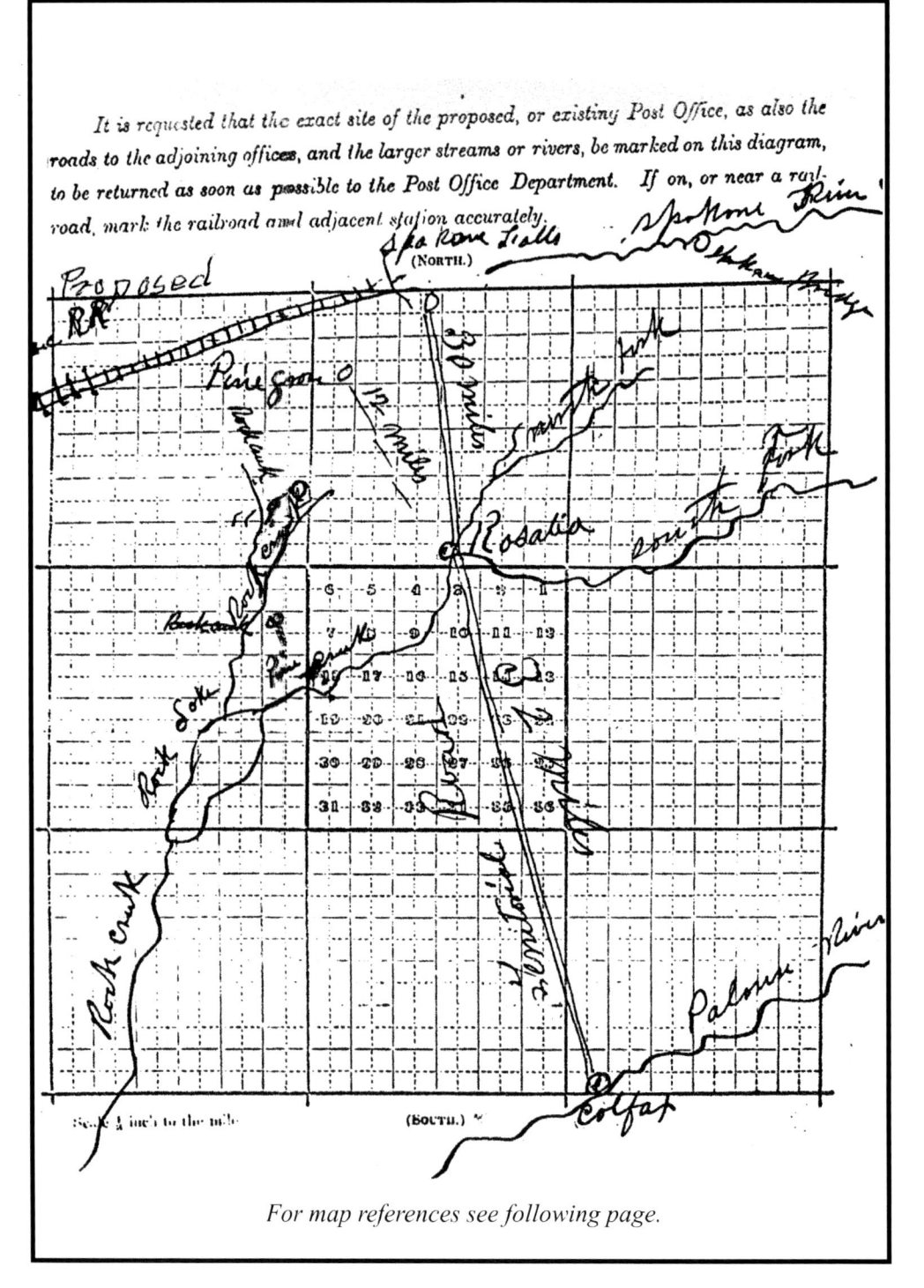

Reference Points:
Location for Post Office - 30 miles south of Spokane Falls on Pine Creek
Nearest Post Office on Mail Route - North - Pine Grove, 12 miles
South - Colfax, 32 miles
Nearest Post Office Off Route - Rock Creek, 10 miles (on Rock Creek, two near Chapman Lake)

Rosalia Post Office (1872) was in Stevens County. The Spokane-Whitman County line was not in existence, but this location was in what today is Spokane County.

Related Area Post Offices (date of beginning of service)
Spokane Bridge - the first post office in the Palouse-Spokane region - 2-26-1867
Rock Creek - 8-31-1871; Colfax - 3-15-1872; Spokane Falls - 6-15-1872; Pine Grove - 7-15-1872; Rosalia - 11-19-1872

Related Geographical Features
Rivers and Streams: Spokane River - north
Palouse River - south
Pine Creek - local
Rock Creek (2) - west

Rosalia Region Roads
(all traveled north from Walla Walla):
Mullan Road - oldest road in the region, headed for Fort Benton, Montana
Territorial Road - headed for Spokane Falls and Colville
Kentuck Trail - paralleled the Territorial Road to Pine Creek, then turned northeast and traveled to Spokane Bridge in the Spokane Valley
Texas Ferry Road - A lesser known road. Traveled north from the Snake River, heading west of Rock Lake and Bonnie Lake to connect with the Mullan Road near the Rock Creek Post Office site just below Chapman Lake.

Property Ownership and General Information Atlases
As settlement expanded and the country filled with people, general atlases began to list many features of interest both to the general public and to businessmen of that time. Now they provide facts and information that are of a great value in connecting and understanding area history.

Atlases would generally cover a specific county and provide a series of maps that would be based on township units. They would show property ownership tracts like farms, also incorporated towns showing the street layout, blocks and individual lots. The road systems would be shown and keyed as to whether they were dirt or improved—improved roads would probably mean they were graded and graveled. Railroad routes would also be mapped. Rural school sites, rural churches and cemeteries would be shown. Their features have now come to be of special interest in preserving a significant part of the local historical scene.

Finally, the atlases would list census figures and details about agricultural activity such as grain production, livestock, orchards, etc. Business activities would also receive coverage. Frequently there would be a liberal selection of individual pictures of homes and prominent citizens in both rural and town areas. Prominent civic or business structures could also be shown that are of special interest to us today in detailing early area growth and development. These atlases are available at local libraries.

Waverly Township as an Example

The map shown here of Waverly Township (Township 21 N Range 44 E) is found in the Chas. Ogle Atlas of Spokane County dated 1912. It is usually referred to simply as the 1912 Atlas. As we look at pioneer history settlement, the Waverly Township gives a fairly typical cross-section of how change was occurring.

Waverly Township had experienced dramatic growth in the thirty-some years since the original survey mapping, and although it was not recognized at that point in time, rural townships in the Palouse had reached their population peak.

By 1912 farm size varied considerably, but the basic 160-acre unit of settlement days was still the norm. Family size might easily run to a dozen or more people. A township would typically have one town; people could travel about five or six miles to do their local shopping and business. Rural school locations were needed on the basis of the fact that children could walk about three miles to attend school. Accordingly, there could be three or four schools in outlying areas. Some rural school enrollments might be as high as thirty or more students. A town school could typically be a hundred or more students. In the early 1900s accredited high schools were just appearing on the scene. Total school-age population could be about 180. Today it would be less than 30. Today, almost all of these students will be living in Waverly.

Area Features

Every community had organizations that publicized optimistic prospects for further growth and business development. The railroads even advertised effectively as far as Europe, painting a picture of unlimited opportunities for immigrants. The atlases of this era had their own role brashly promoting the region.

There was a surprising range of agricultural diversification in the early 1900s. Orchards were a major activity. Most area towns had fruit companies that owned orchards, packing sheds and box factories. These were important assets to the local economy. Many farms had sizeable orchards, as well.

Waverly Township

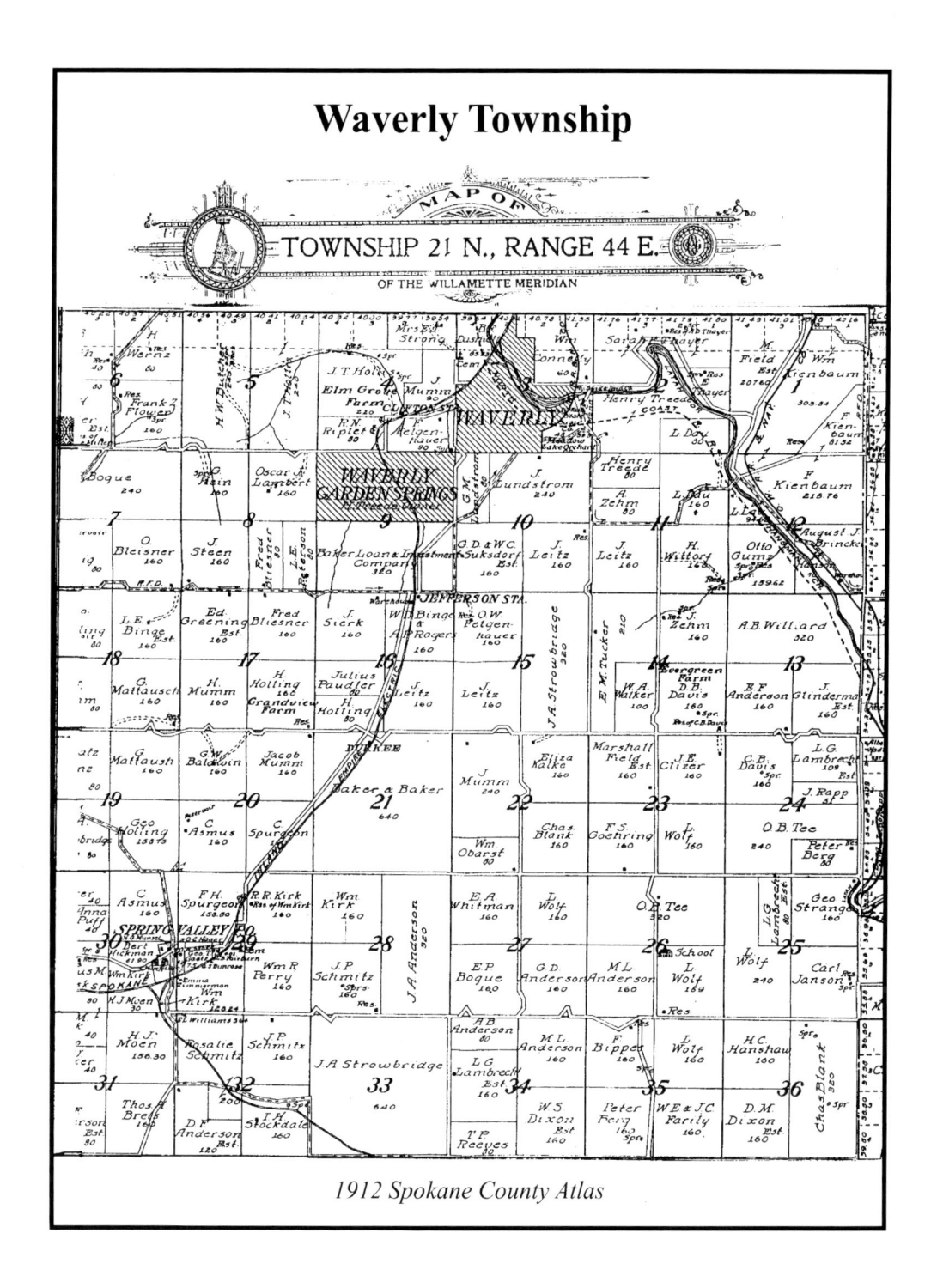

Map of Township 21 N., Range 44 E.
of the Willamette Meridian

1912 Spokane County Atlas

Bi-County Map

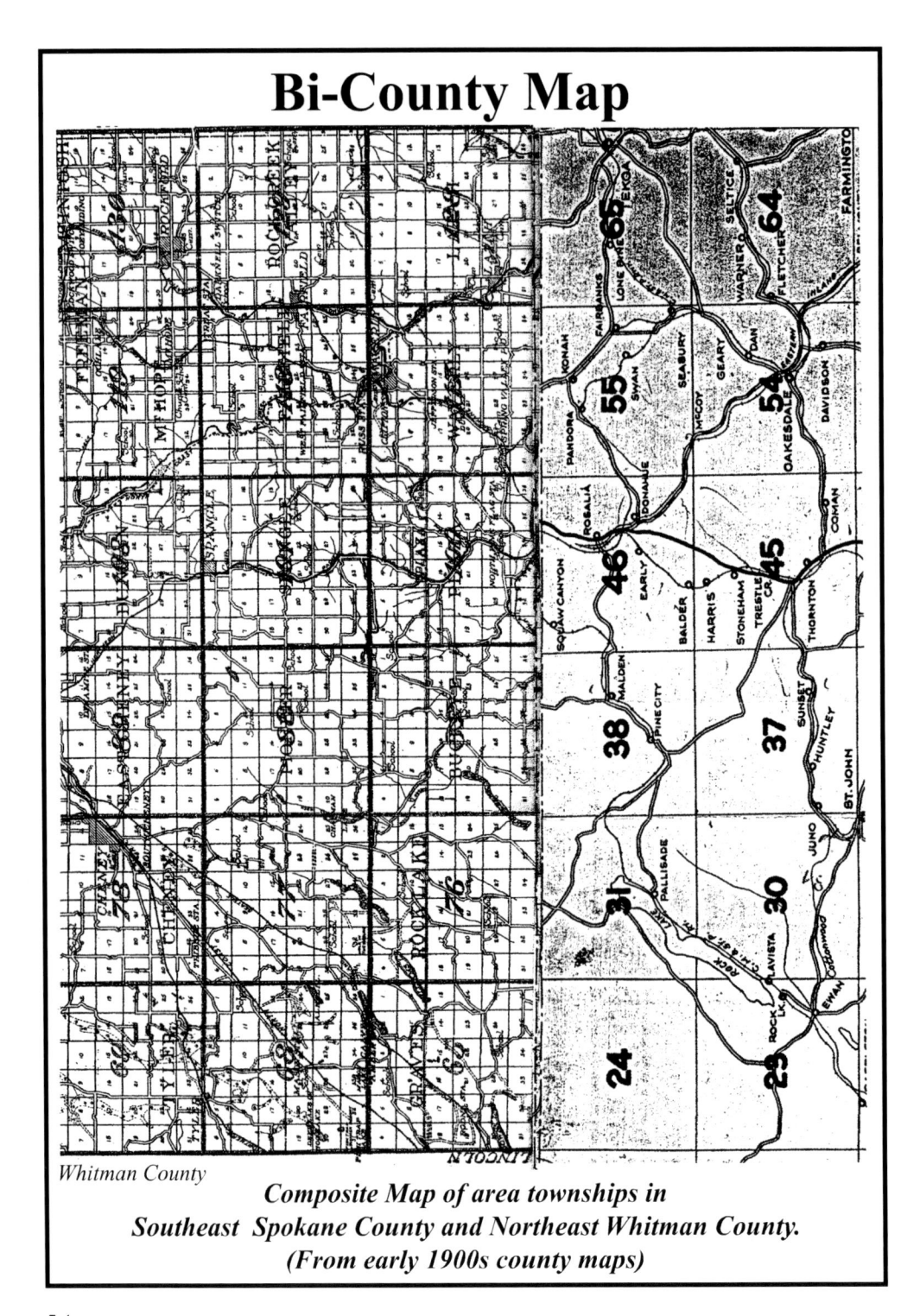

Whitman County

**Composite Map of area townships in
Southeast Spokane County and Northeast Whitman County.
(From early 1900s county maps)**

Dairies were a large scale activity in the north Palouse. Almost every farm would produce milk and cream. Rosalia had a special claim to fame. It had the largest dairy in the nation, with six or seven hundred head of cows and more than fifty employees. Dairy products could be easily shipped to the Spokane markets by rail.

An almost forgotten feature of local farming was a sizeable activity in raising vegetables and row crops such as potatoes. These items would find a market in Spokane and particularly in area mining centers like the Silver Valley. In a similar vein, farm-slaughtered meat was a significant local product that helped make up a broadly diversified agricultural industry. The area was fortunate to have the rail service that made these markets readily available.

Finally, area promotion would come back to the area stalwarts: grains and legumes. Grain storage structures (warehouses), local flour mills and pea seed plants were widespread. They provided jobs that were an important part of the local economy.

All activities in the early 1900s were labor intensive. The large families of this era fit into this mode, especially in the case of farm children, they would have chores to perform at an early age. By the age of ten or twelve, boys normally would be driving teams of horses, and girls would usually work long hours in the house and garden. Family labor was a common, and important, factor in farming success.

A very large number of migrant seasonal laborers came into the Palouse. The large grain harvest crews were a popular part of the historic scene. The intensive labor of the sugar beet industry is mentioned elsewhere in this book. Orchard crews and grain warehouse laborers are other examples of a vibrant part of the local scene.

This was all about to drastically change, with the appearance of the internal combustion engine and as technology ushered in "labor saving" devices. The automobile and the mechanical age changed the rural areas. Increased mobility and the increases in farm size were almost like a death knell to farm towns. Current census figures show another startling development. The population in early times was a young one, age-wise. Now, in addition to being so sparsely populated, rural regions have a very high proportion of older citizens.

Townships Fade into the Sunset

Townships had a key role in area history. They were far more than just a property note on legal documents and land descriptions. Now that important place in local government is almost forgotten. Fitting between school districts and counties, they had an important role in the days when people could not easily go far for the local community services they needed.

Townships had the taxing authority for most of the road building and maintenance. This was a big job involving considerable equipment and manpower. The townships had other areas of local authority. Local livestock control was important, and a "pound master" would be appointed to see that road right of ways were fenced and that livestock did not wander unattended. Liquor and prohibition sentiments were hot local issues. Townships and incorporated towns were separate entities, and "local option" questions made for some interesting laws and for some vigorous debates.

Eventually, the counties took over all the road work and political roles. By the 1960s townships had become mere shadow organizations, and they were phased out of existence. Now their former descriptive information can still be useful, to provide some insight and data that are important reminders of an earlier time.

CHAPTER 6

Early Travel

Early Day Travel Experiences
Travel into the Palouse in early settlement times was likely to be an adventuresome experience. With favorable conditions it could be a pleasant enough endeavor. The rolling topography provided frequent viewpoints over a lush, verdant prairie with unmatched vistas in every direction. The foothills and breaks of the mountains which appeared on the borders added another dramatic dimension to a traveler's sense of awe.

Different seasons brought a great variability to the travel experience. The heat and dust of fall would make for wearisome travel. Snow and freezing cold were sharp companions through the winter. But the real bane of early-day travel would inevitably be the season of the spring thaw and the mud that would accompany it. Mud—ugly, sticky and deep—the most severe test of a traveler's mettle and stamina. Early-day settlers would tell of a four- or five-day endurance trial to travel from Colfax on up into the northern Palouse during the "mud season."

An Early Trip Across the Palouse
The journey of a Commissioner of Immigration on an inspection tour into the area in the 1870s gives an interesting first-hand account of some of the sights and experiences. He was making regular reports to a newspaper at Portland. We join him coming up the Snake River to Almota, which was quite a transportation hub of that time. He found Almota to be "quite a young city...numbering some twenty buildings. A 'hack' line (a multi-seated carriage) runs on the landing of every boat to Colfax; a distance of seventeen miles and a fare of $2.50." He goes on, "I found the assent from the river to be quite objectionable to persons having a heavy load. After walking up the steepest grades and (horses and wagon having stuck in the mud) compelling an unloading of persons and baggage and reloading...the same, and all covered and bespattered with mud, wearied and hungry we arrived (at Colfax) at 2 P.M. having been on the road since early breakfast."

Colfax and Spokane Falls would be his main successive destinations. With regard to Colfax, he ranked it... "in fact the metropolis of the great Palouse country." Preparing to move further north... "we decided to be equestrian (travel via horseback) for the next five or ten days."

"Our first day's ride of fourteen miles brought us to the...homestead ranch of J. S. Davis," (See Mrs. Davis's letter to her children which follows) "known as

57

'Steptoe Station'...He is a fine specimen of many of the noble sons of America. ...From a forty-acre field of wheat he harvested two thousand bushels of grain. Has a fine orchard of apple, pear and plum and all the concomitants of civilization and refinement."

He next traveled on to the home of Mr. Spangle at Pine Grove, 28 miles from Colfax, where the stages from Spokane and Colfax met at this time. "The place was quite promising having a blacksmith shop, cabinet maker's shop, a hotel, store, post office and schoolhouse. Mr. Spangle had lived here for seven years at this date."

The next day he was on to Spokane Falls, which he had expected would be "the place of his golden dreams, excellent climate, matchless beauty of surroundings, immense forests of timber, pine, fir, tamarack, spruce and cedar, magnificent waterfalls just styled as the Niagara of the northwest, the future capital city and emporium of this great inland empire." He found one blacksmith shop, one livery stable, one store, two hotels, one sawmill, one flouring mill, one schoolhouse and several private dwellings.

With regard to the local land, he reported that a vast amount is "worthless for farming purposes. ...It is all 'scabby,' (that is, it has rocky spots in it). In some localities these spots are small, while in other places they cover hundreds of acres..."

The commissioner had seen his travel trials begin when he left the river at Almota. At that point in the trip frustrations began. He concluded, "The conveyances for the accommodation of travel are precarious as to the resultant effects on the hapless traveler. But with all, the journey was interesting, and its thrills and uncertainty made a marked adventure."

'Indian Panics' Created Chaotic Travel Conditions

Few early Palouse residents have a more lasting claim to fame than Mr. and Mrs. James (Cashup) Davis. Cashup's stories are a Palouse country treasury of pioneer experiences. Not too surprisingly, we have a much more limited insight into his wife's life and times, but the experience to be related now is one of the clearest examples of the state of mind of some area people in a time of real turmoil.

I'm not sure how widely this letter has been circulated—it is certainly an interesting window on that particular time. I first saw it in a file at the Whitman County Historical Society in Pullman. It is a poignant record of one of the incidents connected with the Indian scares resulting from the Nez Perce hostilities in 1877.

The letter was written by Mary Ann Davis, who lived with her family near Steptoe Butte (present-day Cashup Flats). The letter was written July 22, 1877 while she was camped on the Tucannon near the Snake River. She and other "refugees" were fleeing south to the Walla Walla area. Here the larger population was expected to provide safety in numbers:

"Dear Children;

I once more take my pencil, for I have no pen. We are fleeing from the Indians. They are broke out and are killing settlers about 40 miles from our house and people are fleeing for their lives. The roads are full of people leaving their homes and everything behind. It's an awful thing. We are on our way to Walla Walla, that is Ed, Mary, Lottie and Charley. We just got our bed and clothing with us, all the rest is behind. Your father and Clarence stayed home to watch the place. Our horses, hogs, and cattle are behind. We got 32 head of horses and colts, and 100 head of cattle and 100 head of hogs. The Indians are killing hogs and cattle by the hundreds and driving off all the horses they can find. We expect to hear of our house being burned and everything destroyed we have. We have 130 acres in with grain and it looks fine. I never saw crops look better, and my garden, we have worked so hard, and have to leave everything for the Indians to destroy. The men are moving their families to Walla Walla and then go back and fight the Indians. Last Saturday they had a fight with General Howard and he killed seventy Indians. I heard the Indians had crossed Clearwater, and more going to fight on Pine Creek or Palouse, [See footnote] that is near our house. Everybody that lives up there has left. ...

The mail goes by here everyday, so you see I can hear if we are all well. ...I don't know what to write to you. It was a dreadful warm day yesterday. We saw dead cattle and hogs on the road and the dogs would stop and howl, and some died. It was the warmest I ever saw. I hope I never see one like this again. This was along the Snake River on the sand. ...O dear, here comes the mail. I can't send the letter now. They had three battles yesterday with the Indians and the Indians beat twice, and butchered the soldiers. And they had a war dance. My paper is full so goodbye."

> Note: The panic and the rumors created many faulty reports. Hostilities were restricted to the area south and east of Lewiston. There were no outbreaks of fighting in the Palouse. How long Mrs. Davis stayed in the Walla Walla region is not reported. Continuing false reports persisted for quite a long time.

A Listing Of Pioneer Roads

It is notable that most of the traffic across the whole Palouse region was in a north-south direction. Many of the topographical features helped this traffic flow—namely the landscape sculpted by the ice age flooding. Still, perhaps the biggest of all the obstacles to traverse was rivers, and their primary direction was east to west. These factors combined to make an interesting setting, and the Snake River really presented a challenge on the way in and out of the Palouse.

The movement of miners traveling to and from the gold mines in Montana and British Columbia provided floods of traffic through the area in the 1860s and 1870s. Then when the settlers began to move into the region to begin ranching and farming, they followed the roads of the mining period.

Of the pioneer trails and roads, the names of the most frequently used crossing the northern Palouse were the Mullan Road, the Texas Road (also commonly called the Texas Ferry Road because of a ferry name on the Snake River), the Territorial Road, the Kentuck Trail and finally the Lapwai Trail.

The Texas Ferry Road and the Lapwai Trail names are not widely recognized

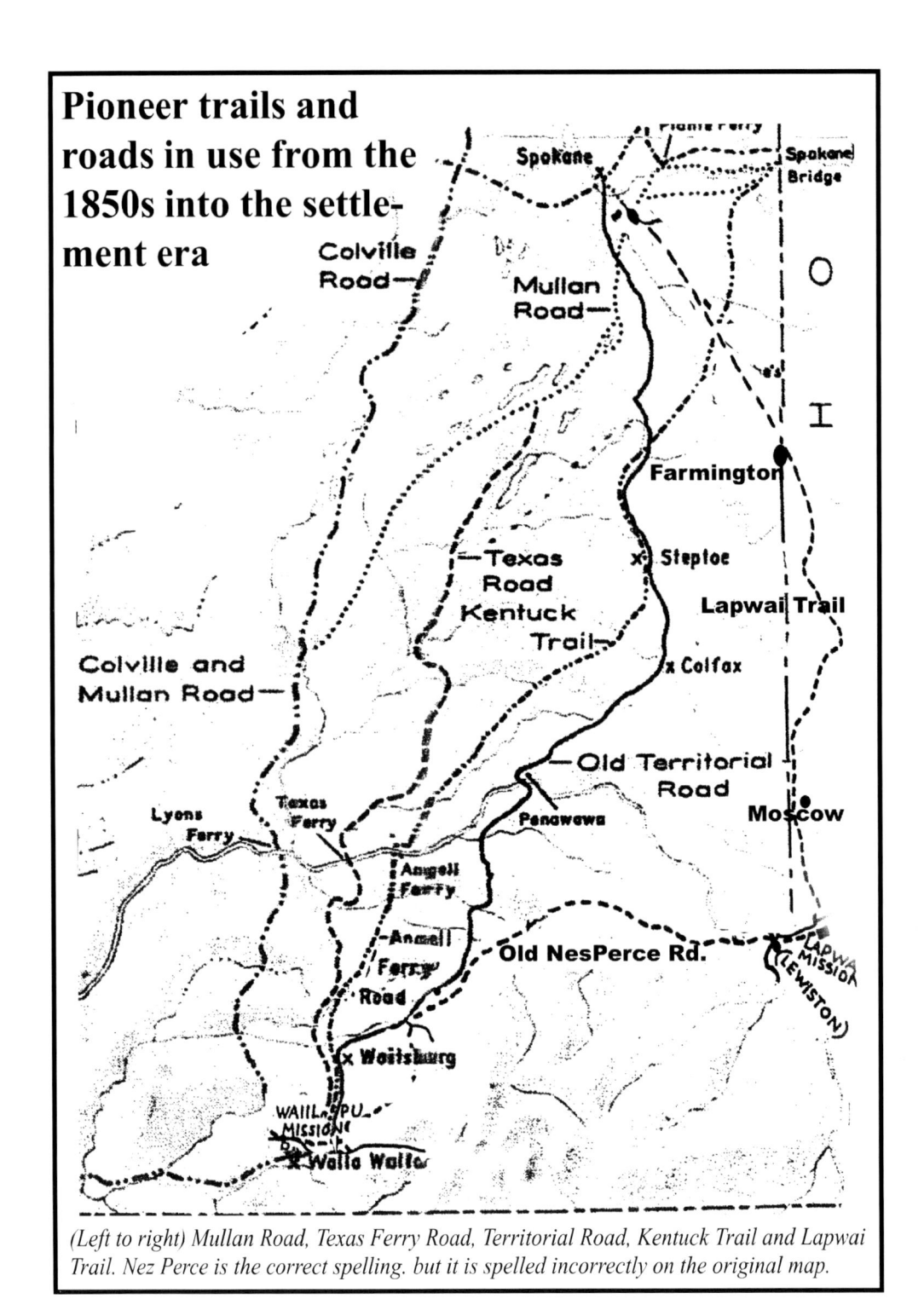

Pioneer trails and roads in use from the 1850s into the settlement era

(Left to right) Mullan Road, Texas Ferry Road, Territorial Road, Kentuck Trail and Lapwai Trail. Nez Perce is the correct spelling. but it is spelled incorrectly on the original map.

today. The Texas Ferry route ended at a junction with the Mullan Road just south of Chapman Lake. The Lapwai Trail was the easternmost route through the Palouse. It is perhaps the most interesting and complex of all the pioneer roads.

The Lapwai Trail had two starting points on the Snake River—one below and one above Lewiston. Then the trail started north, roughly paralleling the present-day Washington-Idaho border as far as Farmington. Here one branch of the trail headed west down Pine Creek. It is notable that this route taken by the Steptoe Campaign to the Rosalia area and their appointment with a historic destiny of defeat by the local Indians. The main route continued up to Hangman Creek. Here traffic could head downstream for Pine Grove (Spangle) and points further to the northwest. Continuing north your destination would be the travel center of Spokane Bridge on the Spokane River near the territorial borders of that time. From Hangman Creek toward the northeast, you could be heading for Coeur d'Alene Lake, the Cataldo Mission, or points far beyond.

Innumerable articles and books have been written about area pioneer travel routes. The following two accounts are just two examples of more local road details.

Lt. John Mullan's Road Across the Northern Palouse

The Mullan Road is one of the oldest and most important pioneer routes in our region. It began at Walla Walla, which was the travel hub and business center for almost every activity throughout a vast part of the inland northwest. There was a great interest by the military and the territorial government to open up a travel route all the way to Fort Benton, Montana. Fort Benton was the head of steamboat travel on the Missouri River at that time.

The official name for this project was the Walla Walla to Fort Benton Military Road. As its name implies, it was built specifically by the government and the Army. It was deemed a national priority to connect the major river systems of the Pacific Northwest with those of the Upper Midwest and to establish a transcontinental link across the northern Rocky Mountains. Some historians like to designate this project as the nation's first transcontinental highway.

This project took quite a long time getting approved by Congress. Lt. Mullan had explored the route, and the Army was anxious to see construction begun. While they were waiting for final approval, smoldering Indian hostilities broke out in this area in 1858. After a troubling beginning, Col. George Wright, in a short and successful campaign, handily ended the conflicts. Mullan served in this campaign with considerable distinction. Finally, in 1859 construction began at Walla Walla and Mullan, with a well-equipped crew of both soldiers and civilians, made a quick start on the project.

Moving northward, he quickly reached the location where the Palouse River meets the Snake. From there he moved up through what is now western Whitman County and on to the Chapman Lake area. Here he turned directly to the east.

The Obscure Route East

Until recently, not very many people were aware of this original road that headed straight east toward the southern end of Coeur d'Alene Lake. People reading about early area history are familiar with the route of the Mullan Road as continuing northerly from Chapman Lake, going up across Moran Prairie and then down to the Spokane Valley, heading for Plante's Ferry near Millwood. Then it followed the Spokane River eastward, passed along the north side of Coeur d'Alene Lake heading to the Cataldo Mission site. But it bears repeating, this was not the route at the time of the road's initial construction.

The original route, upon leaving the Chapman Lake area, traveled east and crossed present-day Highway 195 approximately four miles south of Spangle. It closely followed the watershed boundary between water running south to the Snake River and the water running north into the Spokane River. Its next present-day landmark was that it passed within a stone's throw of the Liberty School between Spangle and Waverly.

From here it made a significant jog to the north, to cross the rugged terrain at the Smythe's Ford crossing of Hangman Creek. This important geographical location was one of the major crossing points of this stream when Hangman Creek was a considerable travel obstacle. It ran a much larger volume of water than today, and at this location the basalt-rimmed canyon was also a considerable barrier. Crossing the stream at this site, Mullan dodged some other rugged terrain near a tributary called Rattler's Run and then broke out again on open prairie. About three miles further, he crossed present-day State Highway 27 just north of Fairfield.

A mile and one-half east of Fairfield a prominent north-south ridge (Hansen's Butte) marks the road's entry into Rock Creek Valley. This grass and timbered ridge was enough of a barrier that it presents some interesting questions of just where Mullan crossed this obstacle.

Most of Mullan's road through this prairie region is now farmland and cultivation effectively erases almost all signs of early roads. Where an area is still in grass and timber there is always some hope that traces of the trail may still be seen. Still, this usually occurs only under the most favorable conditions. Later-day uses, particularly logging or other access roads, decidedly confuse the issue. You can only make judgments based on the known direction of travel and the topography. I have made numerous visits to landowners along this route. Their familiarity with a given location is important for an accurate overview. Almost all of these individuals exhibit a deep interest in this sort of project that has now become a subject of local interest.

The route through Rock Creek Valley is a little more puzzling because of the topography created by a few more local streams and the beginning of broken timber on the way east. A very effective landmark is reached as the route ascends out of the Rock Creek Valley and climbs to a major pass approximately three miles beyond the present-day Washington-Idaho border. When he reached this location, Mullan had a terrific view. Back to the west was the panorama of the valley and the Palouse country; to the east was a dramatic view to Coeur d'Alene Lake and the vast mountain ranges ahead. These would be far more serious obstacles to his road project as he pushed on toward the Cataldo Mission and further east.

Mullan undoubtedly chose this route for his road because of his experience with the Wright Campaign of 1858. Wright had initially dictated treaty terms to the Indians first at the Cataldo Mission. Then he moved on to his second treaty camp on Hangman Creek via the south end of Coeur d'Alene Lake. To Mullan it was familiar ground.

The Route Across the Palouse is Abandoned

Why was this part of the road rerouted after only two years? This route could hardly be negotiated for quite a while in the spring and early summer run-off period. Mud and turbulent waters could be effective road blocks. Mullan soon revised the route to the one we recognize today.

This latter historic road is generously marked with a number of historic monuments. There is only a lonely marker on the original route in an isolated campground in Heyburn Park. It is an excellent interpretive sign with an informative text, a route map and pictures of Mullan and early-day sights. Here the old road can still be seen plainly. Deep wagon ruts down the steep grade to the lake and the old road through huge old trees in the park are still easily seen today. It's too bad this sign isn't at a more accessible location!

The Mullan Road ran approximately six hundred miles and cost $230,000.00. Its use as a military road never met expectations. The route across the mountains was over very difficult terrain. Severe winter snow and storms and bridge washouts and windfalls made it a difficult and expensive road to keep open. Through the mountains it quickly deteriorated into a route only used for pack trains.

The western part of the road continued to be a primary route for supplying travelers and delivering mining goods on a route in and out of the interior northwest. It had a long run in performing this important task and attained a high standing in the region's travel history.

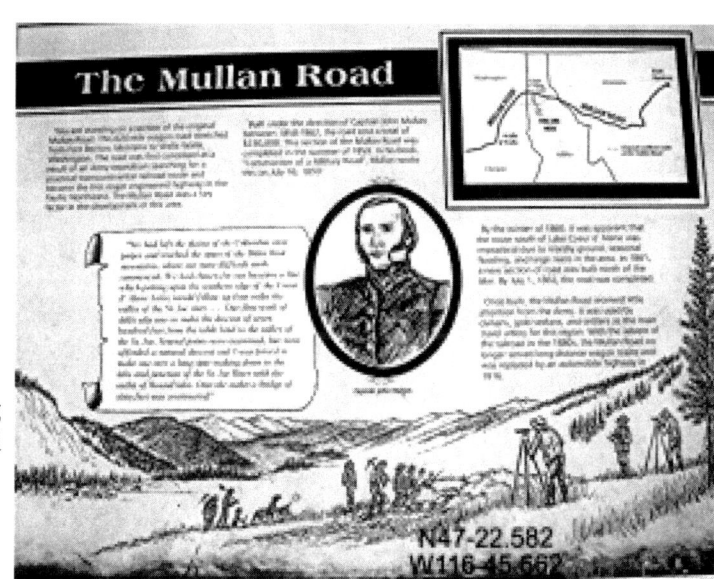

Heyburn Park Interpretive Sign *(Mullan Road Interpretive sign picture: courtesy of Jerry Ingerskie)*

63

The Kentuck Trail

In the northern Palouse, another old-time travel route of particular interest is the Kentuck Trail. It started at the Snake River (near Riparia) and headed up through the eastern Palouse to end in the Spokane Valley near the Idaho border. (Spokane Bridge)

This somewhat unusual name came from the nickname of one of the Snake River ferry operators. He was called "Kentuck Ruark." Ferry operators would advertise in area papesr to encourage use of their particular ferry. Ruark would say that this route, served from his ferry, had excellent water, grass and wood for travelers using this road. In addition, it was a good shortcut because it was "straight as an arrow!" These factors did indeed make it a popular route. The Kentuck Trail had one or two peculiarities—it didn't pass through very many towns, and I don't know if it ever had any stagecoach or mail service along its route. This was unusual.

Old Area Trail Emerges Briefly From the Past

When I was doing some local research several years ago, I was interested to learn the Kentuck Trail ran far enough east that it crossed the Waverly Township on its northwest corner. This fact was shown on the original 1873 township survey map. Another clue I found at the same time was that the ancient trail ran adjacent to the old Prairie View School site in this area.

This, over a period of time, initiated an interest on my part in trying to pinpoint more of this trail's original route through the northern Palouse, especially the part from Pine Creek east of Rosalia and on to the Smythe's Ford crossing at Hangman Creek. This latter point is, of course, the famous site of the Col. George Wright Treaty Camp and the Indian hangings that are commemorated in that stream's name.

I'm sure I've had some local people question my sanity as I've driven around the area asking local landowners if they had any clues or old-time pioneer reports of where this trail might have crossed any present-day roads or other landmarks. Fortunately, sometimes these strange compulsions bear results!

A farmer who lives near Rosalia farms land adjacent to the old Prairie View School. He called me and reported, "You might be interested in some old wagon tracks that we see from time to time in the early summer near the old schoolhouse." This is in cultivated farmland, and the possibility that these old tracks could occasionally still be seen was almost unbelievable! They were quite distinct in the winter wheat crop. Just across a present-day gravel road in a lentil field a distinct change in the crop color was the primary feature that stood out.

There is another neighboring farmer whom I had asked several times about whether he could make any judgments regarding the location of the trail through some particularly hilly land he farms nearby. Now that we had the nearby farm site pinpointed, it was easy to see that the trail went south directly behind his farmstead. Area old-timers remember pioneers talking about Indians traveling through the area along this same route. These facts all seem to connect.

More questions about the trail's route through this area still exist, but there was certainly a sense of satisfaction in this instance on the information that has reemerged. It has provided interesting memories about this particular pioneer road.

Stagecoach Days

No commentary on pioneer travel would be complete without mention of the stagecoach days. This was a means of travel that had a special element of historic romance all of its own, and this romance carried over to the coach driver as well. These remarks will focus on a man who was probably the best known driver in the inland northwest. His name was Felix Warren.

Felix Warren and his father came west via a covered wagon. They had a very eventful trip, filled with adventure and excitement and close escapes from tragedy and Indian attacks. The Warrens settled at Walla Walla in 1865. Felix was twelve years old, but he had a full schedule of caring for a big garden, selling the produce, and helping care for the cattle they had trailed west. Soon the Warren men—a husky boy at that time counted for a man—were farming wheat and raising cattle, but a far more exciting life was in the offing.

By 1873 Felix was packing supplies from Walla Walla to the Kooteney Mines. The accounts of that time state, "It was a trip of 30 to 35 days of long hours of the hardest kind of continuous hard travel. Brushes with desperados and Indians could add elements of danger." After packing all summer, a return to Walla Walla for the winter was a welcome break.

At this point a long-time love affair culminated in marriage. The next year—with help from his father-in-law—the new couple began cattle ranching on the Touchet River. Warren appears to have been too itchy-footed to settle long in one place. He returned to packing and then to running a stage route from Almota to Colfax in 1875. In a particularly dramatic move he became an Army scout in the Nez Perce War in 1877 and also the Bannack Indian War in 1878. Both of these adventures were filled with myriad dangers and close calls. Warren then returned to Almota and took up a career for which he was to become most famous.

A friend's account tells, "He stocked and operated an area stage line with all the challenges that entailed; unimproved and almost impossible roads, roads with ruts deep with dust in midsummer and deep mud in winter and spring. There were few bridges—all streams possible being forded, and everywhere dangerous grades and tortuous curves to test a driver's skills."

Felix Warren experienced the full range of weather, physical obstacles and human frailty and human virtue. Through it all, Warren was a premiere example of the "Western Man" marked with ability, daring and skill. He continued to look for opportunity over distant horizons, running a wide range of stage and freighting endeavors.

This icon of the west was an impressive figure—tall, strong and athletic. As time passed, his goatee, moustache and hair turned white. He wore a large-brimmed, high-crowned Stetson. Warren had the style and bravado of a showman, and he relished this role as he grew older. He seemed to be comfortable and somewhat proud of his status as the ultimate frontiersman.

Warren was unabashedly proud of his skills as a "linesman." He received rave reviews when he appeared at a Chicago Exposition driving a forty-horse hitch in a western show exhibition. Even more notable was an event in 1926. Air mail was being introduced into the Spokane area, with Pasco being the distribution point. It was decided to commemorate this new technology by comparing it with the original stage coach delivery and with all the memories that entailed. A reenactment of the old method of stagecoach delivery would be reason for a region-wide celebration, and who better for the driver than Felix Warren?

The stagecoach left Spokane with huge fanfare and started south. The route went via Spangle, Rosalia and Oakesdale. A zigzag route through the Palouse gave many towns an opportunity to bring out huge crowds, listen to speeches, take pictures and have all the local news reporters present. Local dignitaries would be permitted to ride the stage between towns for one last ride in a conveyance and a style that was now only a note in history.

In the 1930s Warren's health began to fail. His death occurred in January of 1937 near Almota. His funeral and burial were at Lewiston. A biographer said, "It was his kind who had the spirit and courage necessary to go where others hesitated to go—to pioneer so that others could follow.

Some Local Railroad Histories

Railroads were a primary economic engine in the area as settlement times gave way to full development. The Oregon-Washington Railroad and Navigation Company (O.W.R. & N.) was the first railroad into the region. It came up through the eastern Palouse. It became part of today's Union Pacific Railroad. The Spokane and Palouse line that was to become the Northern Pacific was soon to follow, selecting routes just a little farther west. Then another later arriving, and unusual railroad, became a Palouse country symbol, and we will look at it more closely.

The Palouse Region Electric Railroad

This map highlights the "local services" aspect of this rail line showing the many local stops and other names that made this line a special feature in the Palouse region. (From Inland Empire Railroad Historical Society)

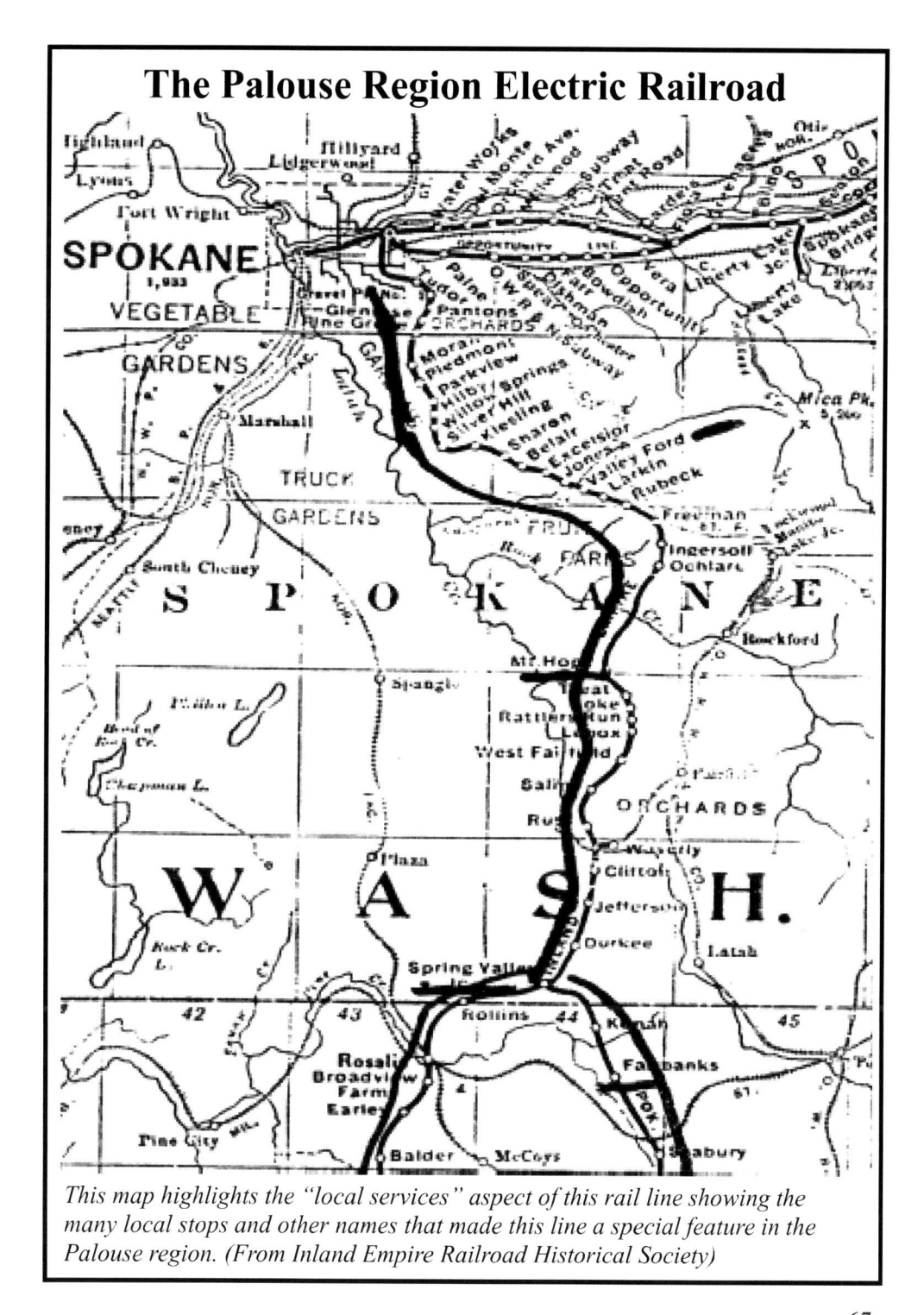

The Spokane and Inland Empire Railroad was the offshoot of suburban electric rail lines in the Spokane area. Many people felt that the Union Pacific and the Northern Pacific were not giving Palouse country residents good service, so several Spokane area business leaders involved with the electric commuter rail system saw this as an opportunity. They thought the growing population of that era and the fertile farmland would make an ideal business venture for an electric railroad. By 1905 they were ready to initiate a plan of action.

This line would begin at a large, impressive terminal building where the Spokane City Library is located today. From here the Palouse branch headed southeast and out over Moran Prairie. Waverly and its sugar beet factory were one of the immediate goals. The owners also visualized commuter communities at places like Valleyford and Freeman.

Just a little south of Freeman the new rail line faced a very large and a very

Rock Creek Trestle. (Courtesy of the Southeast Spokane County Historical Society)

special construction project. They had to build a massive bridge across Rock Creek canyon. Unusually large construction crews were pressed into service, and the Rock Creek trestle project received wide publicity. At that point in time it was the largest and highest trestle to be constructed, with a major curve engineered into the structure.

The railroad was state of the art technology in a number of very important ways. Electric power was coming into wide use for city transit lines, but adapting it to full-scale passenger and freight service was another large step. The railroad ran on AC current taken off an overhead wire. The passenger cars were driven by four 100-

horsepower motors at each set of wheels. The freight engines were powered by banks of motors that turned out 1200 horsepower.

An interesting feature of the electric current was that it had to be boosted or 'stepped up.' This had to be done at about twenty-mile intervals. These "substations" had an impressive array of electrical components housed in square-shaped, two-story high brick buildings. They were an interesting landmark on the local scene. At least two of these buildings still survive in the northern Palouse.

The passenger car furnishings and depot facilities were all first class. The cars were handsomely furnished with wicker seats, and the walls were trimmed with hardwoods and glazed art glass. Ornately painted ceilings and parquet or rug-covered floors were incorporated into an optimum in style and comfort.

The local depots were built of brick and had a significantly more impressive architectural style than the typical wood depots of the other regional lines. At Spring

Spring Valley Depot. (Courtesy of Pasey Family)

Valley, the major junction where lines branched to Moscow and to Colfax, a large two-story depot was a highlight. It was budgeted at a lavish $5,000.00 cost and was the show place of the area. The owners of this railroad were committed to the best of design and appearance.

The timing and big investment of this project was not to be favorable for success. The emphasis on style and quality had a high price tag, and revenues never reached expectations. The popularity of the new automobiles only added to the financial crunch.

The line went through ownership changes, the demise of passenger service and the inevitable decline in freight business which was to be the final death knell.

Jay P. Graves

The primary organizer of this railroad was a man by the name of Jay P. Graves. He had accumulated a fortune in mining, and then he turned to an interest in Spokane real estate with even greater success. Later projects like this railroad venture generated huge losses. In his later years he was reduced to living in very modest circumstances.

Like many self-made successful men, Graves was dogmatic and opinionated. In his original Spokane business endeavors he had worked closely with the Washington Water Power Company (now Avista) who originated electric-powered city transit in Spokane. He worked hand in hand with them for years.

When he began planning forays into electric railroad operations Graves had a major falling out with WWP. In an example of big-time spite, he built the Nine Mile Falls dam to supply his own electricity. This had another interesting connection to local history. Nine Mile Falls dam appears to be the first dam (shortly after 1905) to block salmon migration on the Spokane River and on up Hangman Creek. This particular claim to fame is seldom remembered today.

Although its service was relatively short-lived, the electric railroad had an important impact on the Palouse region, and it occupies an interesting place in area history.

The Northern Palouse's 'Mystery' Railroad

In the early 1900s building new rail lines had many of the aspects of a full-blown fad. Most railroad tycoons were exceptionally aggressive and very jealous of their peers. They would literally move mountains to compete with rival railroads. Much of this competition was poorly thought out. Initial rivalry and jealousy could often lead to some interesting second thoughts on just how practical hasty plans actually were.

In this time period a railroad was planned and surveyed, and construction was actually started on a railroad up Hangman Creek valley. Details on this project have always been a little sketchy. Over a period of time there were some obscure references among older area residents about this railroad. Mainly they were stories about a mysterious abandoned right of way where pine trees now grow seventy or eighty feet high.

These old road bed sites along Hangman Creek were built in unconnected sections—probably because of the rugged terrain. Extensive rock removal and bridging of the stream would have been major hurdles. There is no evidence that any bridge building actually occurred, and this would be a primary reason for the piecemeal pattern of construction. The last section of right of way built was just a few miles below Waverly.

For many years the questions about who started this project, where the railroad was going and what caused its abandonment all seemed to be unanswered. Then a closer look at the Spokane County 1912 Atlas provided some tantalizing clues. The name of the proposed railway was the North Coast Railroad. This was an important regional railroad company of that era, and this would be a branch line from Spokane, probably heading for Lewiston. The project was an effort of a Spokane railroad promoter by the name of Robert Strahorn. He was an agent and a front man for Edward Harriman who was one of the really important national railroad tycoons. Strahorn was one of the most important figures on the local railroad scene. He and his wife became part of Spokane's moneyed aristocracy, and they built one of the biggest early-day mansions in Browne's Addition. This home was the site where the M.A.C. museum now stands.

In the booming environment of the early 1900s all sorts of rail projects were envisioned and planned. After a realistic appraisal, a number of these efforts were shut down. That was the case with this Hangman Valley project.

The heyday of railroading certainly created many events and stories that are an interesting part of our regional travel history.

Railroads

Railroads have their claim to an important place in the development of the west and our region in particular. The factors of the great distances to overcome in access for the final large waves of settlers to arrive in the area, the increasing need to bring in manufactured supplies and the need to access markets for local products, these forces all combined into a crucial role for the railroads.

It has not been widely recognized that because of a special set of features of geography, natural resources and settlement patterns, the Palouse region had one of the most elaborate and comprehensive rail networks in existence anywhere.

The accompanying map shows the vast rail system that accompanied the region's growth. By 1910 Spokane was a railroad hub with five transcontinental lines. Additional regional lines pushed to every corner of the Palouse.

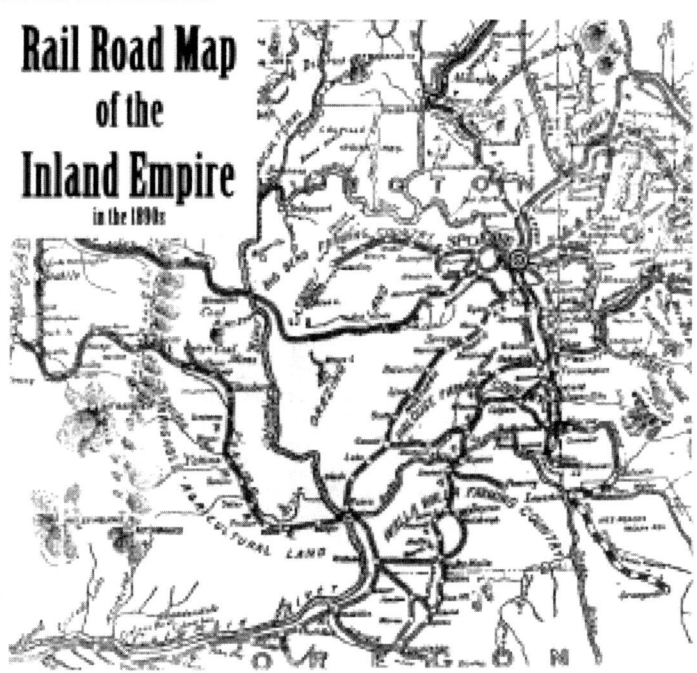

(From Inland Empire Railroad Historical Society)

71

CHAPTER 7

"Promoting" The Palouse Region

As settlement got underway, there was a major effort to build up the population and promote development. This occurred on both a local and a regional scale.

In the 1890s the following article was part of a Spokane Falls promotional effort that was widely publicized:

The Palouse Country - Most Fertile in Soil and Most Abundant in Crop

The Ideal El Dorado For The Farmer, Husbandman And Stock Raiser—in Scenery, Climate And Productiveness Almost Unequaled—its Possibilities And Probabilities

The Palouse farming district is the Mecca where the most fertile soil awaits the busy hand of the farmer and where an abundant crop and a magnificent yield are the rewards of his labor and toil. Much has been written and published about the agricultural qualities and inexhaustible resources of this section of the Northwest, but fabulous as these reports may sound to the ears of those who are not acquainted with the real value of this agricultural section of the Northwest, the subject has not been exaggerated. But it is a fact beyond contradiction that the Palouse farming region is the finest agricultural region of the entire Pacific Northwest, if not of the world.

As to the soil, to say that it is rich and fertile is picturing its value in the very mildest form. It is very deep, running from three to seven feet, and of that rich, loose loam which is so productive to the farmer. Originally the ground was covered with a very dense and luxuriant growth of bunch grass.

The yield of wheat is never lower than 25 and frequently as high as 60 bushels to the acre, although from 35 to 40 bushels per acre is the average yield. It will at once be evident that this average yield to an acre is higher than in any other section of the United States.

Other states may suffer severely from the drought in the summer or the frost in the winter, but the extreme seasons of the year have never had a damaging effect upon the crops of the Palouse country. The farmer who cultivates his land in that favored section of the Northwest need fear no failure. He may have one year a better crop than the other, but he is always assured of an abundant harvest. The yield of oats and barley is equally satisfactory. While the soil is admirably adapted to the growing and cultivation of all farm products, the Palouse country is properly destined to become a great crop area. The rolling hills rise majestically over the valleys and plateaus covered with bountiful crops. The climate is such that it might be described as glorious. Mild winters, timely rains, a long growing season—these attributes make it a place where industry and effort will yield prosperity and plenty.

Just a little later, local farm towns and communities had advanced to the place where they had their own Chambers of Commerce and Commercial Clubs. These organizations were rampant boosters for their communities and areas. Their enthusiasm for more population and businesses was limitless.

About 1905 Rosalia's Chamber of Commerce put together a publication to promote their area. They began by connecting to their most historic and best known event—the Steptoe Battle of 1858. This was a way to spotlight their community. After they had described that historic connection, they turned to highlight the present and the future outlook. In the style of that day, flowery language and prose was one of their promotional techniques of choice.

An example of this: *"The world renowned deltas of the Nile or the bottoms of the Mississippi do not surpass the Palouse Hills in fertility. Well farmed land will consistently raise 35 bushels per acre, with even occasional production up to 45 bushels per acre. The rainfall and the temperature are agreed to create an incomparable climate."*

Finally, the local citizens were lauded as progressive and hard working, with examples of the success that those endeavors could bring. A number of these farmers and businessmen were profiled, along with pictures of their prosperous farms, homes and town business structures.

This booklet concluded by hoping many readers of this "honestly phrased" report would become residents and "enjoy the privileges of living in a live, prosperous, law-abiding and united community where they could fully enjoy the benefits of the culture, convenience and every advantage."

Inland empire of the Northwest As the cover of this promotional pamphlet suggests, wheat farming was closely linked to the image of the Inland Empire. By permission of Cheney Cowles Museum/Eastern Washington State Historical Society, Spokane, Washington.

Fairfield's Commercial Club Promotion

Within a year or two, nearby Fairfield published a similar promotional write-up. It was an effort of the Fairfield Commercial Club. This booklet was more elaborate, incorporating color and more professional pictures and text. The local railroad cooperated, as well as Sunset Magazine. Undoubtedly, they both contributed expertise and financing to this project. This production highlighted prospects for a much diversified agriculture. Orchards were developing into a major local endeavor. Prospects were fully explained and unlimited benefits were expected. Their development would be a centerpiece of a more diverse agricultural industry.

Creation of a larger population was expected, with a more intensive land use and labor force. Establishing orchards, fruit packing plants and box factories and allied businesses for other specialty crops was a centerpiece of optimism. This was the time of the sugar beet boom mentioned elsewhere in this book, and vegetable and flower seeds were expected to be major area products. With the skill and efforts of Col. E. H. Morrisson (mentioned elsewhere in this book) specialty crops were seen as guaranteeing a bonanza to the region.

A commentary in this booklet lauded Morrison as the region's own Luther Burbank—a plant breeder who had achieved national fame. Morrison was credited with operating the largest seed farm in the Pacific Northwest. Finally, Morrison's efforts to develop and promote a dry pea industry were fully and duly noted. Fairfield's advertising and promotional efforts made the following statement:

'A Land Of Plenty'

Owing to its fertility, the variety of products which may be grown, its nearness to market and its good climate, the Fairfield, Washington, district is destined to become thickly settled. For many years it has been known as a grain growing section. It is adapted to the growth of every product of the temperate zone. Crop failures are unknown. The testimony of those who have engaged in tilling the soil here is to the effect that every effort has been rewarded. Fairfield sends out this booklet as the first advertisement of its productive lands, and with the publication there is given an invitation to the man in search of a location to look into conditions here. Careful inquiry as to what the land will produce and what the grower receives for his crops and further inquiry as to markets and transportation facilities are asked. These taken in connection with the low prices at which holdings may be secured are arguments in favor of the territory immediately adjacent to Fairfield. A careful reading of the pages which follow is asked. Facts alone are presented. The Commercial Club of Fairfield stands back of every statement made and is ready to substantiate the testimony of the individual who is quoted along any line. Health, wealth and prosperity are in store for those who come, even as these have been the heritage of the settler of former years.

Grain Farming's 'Staying Power'

The northern Palouse did have a remarkable diversity of agriculture for several decades at the turn of the last century. However, orchards were subject to weather extremes. Frosts in the spring and severe winter weather that could kill fruit trees made fruit a high-risk endeavor. Increasingly wide scale irrigation was becoming more competitive venues for both fruit and row crops. With these conditions existing, a concentration on grain farming became the norm, and the bounty of these crops became even more the long-lasting hallmark of the region.

Early day farming scenes

The "Traction Engine" was a harbinger of technology and large scale farming.

The "Family" farm.

Additional farming scenes

A "Farming Bee" demonstration in the Fairfield-Waverly area.

A harvest scene in the Idaho part of the Palouse.

Resources: Mining And Oil Exploration

Early Day Mining in the Northern Palouse

The history of the Palouse country might not seem to have much of a direct connection with the mining business. Many of us are aware that there was a large movement of early day miners and early day mining supplies through the region on the way to mining fields further afield in Idaho, Montana and British Columbia. The fame of these "strikes" would spread far and wide, and mining was a dramatic lure and attraction in pioneer times.

When the reality of the hardships and slim chances to hit a "big bonanza" sank in, many disillusioned miners decided to switch to the more settled life of a rancher or a farmer. As a result, many early day area families had a connection to mining, and the ideas of a "hot" mining property still had quite a lot of appeal to the locals.

I remember being quite surprised when I began studying some old community history accounts about the northeast corner of the Palouse that told how widespread local mining exploration was here close to home. A good many of the faults that trail off of the western slopes of the nearby mountains had quartz ledges at various locations. Traces of gold and silver were not hard to find. Soon prospect holes and mine tunnels were widespread.

Some of the old local histories give extensive listing of various properties that had mining endeavors on a large number of area buttes. In some places deep vertical shafts were sunk, often with lateral shafts following some tempting mineral veins.

In other locations, tunnels were dug horizontally into hillsides. These would run considerable distances—also looking for elusive veins with gold or silver content. Some of these operations were large enough to employ ore cars and a track system. Almost all required heavy timbers for tunnel bracing and supplying mining timbers was quite a business.

Today most of these old mine sites are collapsed or water filled. For a long time they were places where local adults would warn away inquisitive kids, but now most of them are hardly recognized.

In the early 1900s Waverly had an assay office. This supports the accounts of how widespread mineral investigations were. It is interesting to note that even in more recent times, someone will still drum up some optimism and revive a prospecting effort—usually efforts that rather quickly fade away again!

Over time many samples were assayed, but sufficient gold or silver were not found to be profitable. Some interesting stories are told about efforts to "salt" mines and mount bogus stock-selling schemes. Most of these stories are now in the realm of area folklore.

'Practical' Mining

Clay mining is an effort that has had a large degree of success. In pioneer times many area towns had associated brick factories. Pottery factories also were an interesting area business.

The real success story of mining-type activity in this region would have to be the local basalt rock and gravel quarries. We tend to take them for granted, but in terms of economic value they have probably been the area's single most important mineral resource. A good rock quarry site is not very glamorous, but it still fills an important need that we frequently fail to appreciate.

Oil Gushers?

Gold and silver ore were not the only mineral objects in the area. Some oil and gas exploration was done between 1905 and 1910. Oil exploration has had its days of excitement in the North Palouse. There have been long-lasting debates and speculation over oil prospects. Whether the area has the geologic structure for oil is questioned even today. So far promotional hype, stock promotions and "dry holes" have been the only result.

'Will Sink Test Wells'

(From the Rosalia Citizen, 1907) The testing of the gas and oil prospects along Pine Creek between Rosalia and Pine City is now practically assured. The Pine Creek Gas and Oil Company, which was formed about two months ago for the purpose of testing the gas and oil prospects in this district, has been making an active canvas for stock subscriptions and met with encouraging success.

The company plans to sink two wells, the estimated cost of which is placed at $10,000. The wells are to be sunk to a 2000-foot level and there are many who believe that a pay streak will be encountered nearer the surface. Local farmers and businessmen and farmers in the vicinity of Pine City desire a thorough test of the gas and oil prospects and are subscribing liberally for the stock. More than half of the necessary cash subscriptions have already been secured, and considerable more has been promised. Ten thousand dollars is considerable amount to invest in a prospect, but the people feel that it is worth that sum to have the question of "oil, or no oil" definitely settled.

The company proposes to purchase a drilling outfit and place a man in charge. It will be remembered that some three years ago when several companies were formed in Spokane for the purpose of testing the gas and oil prospects in this district the undertaking was a rank failure, simply because the drillers were incompetent and unable to reach much more than the common water level depth. The company will guard against a repetition of this performance by retaining its own drilling force and letting no contracts. It is believed that the company will be able to start drilling as soon as harvest is over.

August 1908 Fairfield Standard

That the geological formation penetrated by the oil drill now being operated at Lenox—two and one-half miles northwest of Fairfield-is the best oil-bearing formation known is widely acknowledged. This is the statement made by a party of Spokane men, including W. S. Sims who is a geologist and oil expert. He was formerly connected with Standard Oil Company for many years.

For all the optimism, these drilling ventures fell flat. The Standard Register was to note that quite a bit later in the 1930s oil drilling optimism appeared on the scene north of Rockford in the Manito area. Results were no more successful than before. (Maybe with today's oil prices we should try again!)

Surprising Mining Ventures

One of the special bonuses of researching area history is when it involves people sharing rare and interesting information about forgotten events. Good examples of this are several pictures that have resurfaced, connecting to local early-day mining activity.

A Mine on Waverly Butte

Waverly Butte mining operation in the background on top of the butte. (Photo from Braman family).

The size and extent of this operation, the apparent amount of investment and effort that would have been expended, and the fact that it has almost been forgotten make this an item of special interest.

There have been a few stories of local mining activities by people who were involved with the Waverly sugar beet factory. Some of the foremen and management level personnel seemed to make this a major second involvement. The reappearance of this picture is quite overwhelming today. It seems strange that some of us who had relatives in the local area never heard them mention this extensive a mining development. The fact that mining never developed into a long-term successful part of the local scene seems to have allowed it to slip from memory. Today we can only wish that it would have been a better documented part of local history.

A Mining Expedition Leaves Latah

Another picture that provides a window to past mining ventures comes from the Latah area. At this point Latah was apparently a staging point for area people going to prospect or work mining properties in the St. Joe River area.

The picture shows riders and their pack string assembled in front of the Latah Bank. This building is the present entrance and customer service area of today's AmericanWest Bank. Some of the men in this picture are still remembered and identified.

Many other towns along the eastern edge of the Palouse benefited from being supply centers for mining ventures in the pioneer era. Large-scale mining efforts in the Silver Valley and the Hoodoo region on the upper Palouse River provided important markets and business stimulus in the Palouse.

The prospectors before leaving Latah. (Photo from Pruett family).

CHAPTER 8

Almost Forgotten Places

There were towns and places that accompanied early settlement that today only exist in fading memories. The first settlers would not travel far to try and secure their basic services so towns and communities were close together. These places would typically start with a post office and maybe a store. A school and whatever else would meet local needs would then follow. Often the schoolhouse would be the location for the first church services and community meetings. On occasion a church would be built out in the open country and the rural one-room schoolhouse became a common feature throughout the region.

A little later the railroads gave rise to more towns as they accompanied regional growth. We now know that boom and growth the railroads generated was not to be long lived and consolidation and technology led to a demise of business and community activity. Many places withered away and died. Here is a listing and a brief record of some of these bygone places.

First Pioneer Places

Hangman Creek and Alpha—Elsewhere in this book we have several references to one of the area's very first pioneers—Major R.H. Wimpy. His home was the location for the "Hangman Creek Post Office." Before long, it is said that some of the local ladies decided this was too gruesome and undesirable a name and the post office was given the name of Alpha—which as many of us know means "the first." This seemed very appropriate for one of the earliest of post offices.

Curlew—was an interesting little early day place in Rock Creek valley. It had an early day post office and school. It was on an early mail and stage route but it rather quickly faded away when Fairfield, about three miles west, kicked into gear with the coming of the railroad in 1888.

Curlew got its melodious name from a local bird that frequented the grassy prairies of yore. Regrettably neither the bird nor the place survived very long. Poems and lyrics about the Curlew and its vibrant song were a popular subject in pioneer literature. Today they can still bring us just a little connection to the past.

Duncan—was a "little" town down in Hangman Creek canyon below its junction with Rock Creek. It had a post office, store, and a large dance hall that was a major landmark until it burned down. A gas station appears to have survived by being remodeled into a residence.

Pine Grove—was the predecessor to Spangle. It was an important early day post office and stage stop. William Spangle plotted a new town a few miles southeast. The railroad came there and Pine Grove is now just another faintly remembered name.

Lockwood—was a post office north of Rockford on the Milwaukee railroad. When it closed in 1903, the mail went to Rockford.

Setters—a location across the state line east of Rockford. It is well toward the northeast corner of the Palouse. It had a store and a post office. There are still grain elevators and a bluegrass seed plant. Just a little farther east there are several old sawmill/logging camp town sites. They have a rather marginal connection to the Palouse, but they are of great interest to people with an affection for the early day forest industry.

Darknell—a trading post-store. This is a really obscure site east of Fairfield, almost at the Idaho State line and about a quarter mile north of Truax (Plummer) road. Darknell was a stagecoach stop and trading site—especially for the local members of the Coeur d'Alene tribe who lived in the area. Darknell is not listed in the early day postal records—which seems a little surprising. It might have been overlooked because of the state line boundary survey questions mentioned elsewhere in this book.

A particularly interesting account of pioneer times here comes to us from Mrs. Clara Darknell. From near Spangle, she recalls walking the last ten or twelve miles to their new home site following Indian trails. Rockford was only a sawmill site. Colfax was the nearest trading point, "it took three days to make the trip with a team. There was a post office at Hangman Creek where we went for our mail once a week."

Like many pioneer women Clara Darknell had a considerable fear and apprehension of the local Indians. She vividly remembered one time at the Darknell store when some Indians took a fancy to her son Ralph and offered to buy him. He was then a handsome, red-headed three year old. Her reaction—terse and sparsely worded—was the equivalent of today's, "No way!"

Mrs. Darknell concluded her story with a notable commentary:

"There were times when we were afraid we could not make a living here. The first wheat we raised frosted before harvest, but we stayed with it and made good. When I see how young people now start out in life with all the modern conveniences and luxuries, I always think of how we started, with all the loneliness, homesickness, privations, etc. I never wrote home and told how homesick I was. It took $300 to bring us to Washington and we had so many things to buy. Had no

money to go back, and would not send home for money, as my father was a regular pioneer and did not have much sympathy for quitters."

> *Editor's note: This is one of the stories from the Standard Register at the time of the Territorial Centennial. It includes the comment that Mrs. Darknell, "wrote this illuminating and succinct account when she was eighty years old."*

A Little Later In Time

Fairbanks—a Whitman County location. It came into existence with the building of the electric railroad line (the Spokane and Inland Empire R.R.) into the Palouse. It had a post office, store, school and some local residents. Today it is still the site of a group of grain elevators that preserve its name. Its' schoolhouse still partly survives—having been converted into a storage building.

Spring Valley—Just a little farther north was another little place that began with the electric railroad. The following story (by Glenn Leitz) appeared in the *Palouse Magazine* in 2003:

Last landmark at Spring Valley to Fall

In the horse and buggy days Spring Valley became a bustling little community when the Spokane-Inland Empire Railroad pushed down into the Palouse between 1905 and 1908. Until then Spring Valley was only the location of a one-room community school. Now this site was to be a major railroad junction. One set of tracks went on southwest toward Rosalia and Colfax—the other headed southeast to Moscow, Idaho.

Soon a grand two-story brick depot was erected, along with warehouses and facilities for a section crew. Several stores emerged on the scene—one with a gas pump and a post office. A hotel and a harness shop were soon added. A modern schoolhouse was constructed and in a short period of time, a peak attendance of forty-some students required an expansion.

The final building to round out this little town was a large and attractive church. In that little rural setting its steeple and bell tower, along with fancy and decorative windows, made it quite a showplace.

By the late 1920's the local population was in a marked decline and church services ended. A Sunday school and a ladies aid society kept active for a few more years. The school closed in 1939. The store and post office closed by 1945. Eventually the church was converted to a barn. A line of cow stanchions became one of the main features of the church basement. That usage also faded away. Next the bell tower was removed to facilitate the installation of a sheet metal roof and the building became a storage barn.

Over time the building became more weather beaten. Even the metal roof began to loosen from the onslaughts of the wind. Few people driving by would ever surmise the building's original appearance and function.

Time has now decreed the useful life of the building has passed; there is only a sad and final requiem—the demolition has begun (2003)! The last vestige of a once vibrant little town is gone. Now only the ubiquitous grain elevators will preserve any vestige of a once thriving community.

Mount Hope and the Mount Hope Church and Cemetery

Mount Hope—about five miles west of Rockford is a community that traces its origins back to the 1890's. It really hit its stride with the building of the electric rail line in the early 1900's. It became the center for a variety of businesses, a large school, and a railroad depot and one of the "brick power houses" that was part of the required technology for the railroad at about twenty mile intervals. This structure still survives today and has been remodeled into an attractive home.

Mount Hope eventually succumbed to the "small farm town syndrome." It did survive with an active store and post office longer that most of the other little towns in that category. Today Mount Hope is within an easy commuting range to Spokane and the Spokane Valley. New houses are being built in the area and the Mount Hope community seems to be assured of survival.

The origin of the Mount Hope name has come down as part of local history. At an early community gathering the settlers were asking, "What shall we call our community?" One of the oldest of the group spoke up, reminding them of the mountains in the distance and how it had taken great courage to come west and not turn back. "We must ever be strong in our hope that we shall make good and strongly resolved that nothing shall prevent us from going on and becoming an established community, ever mindful and grateful of our blessings. Let's call it Mount Hope." Great applause greeted his suggestion, for the name suited them all.

The story of the "little white church" standing at the crossroads of Mount Hope is a dramatic account. At this location a church and cemetery date back to 1886 when a local pioneer deeded a little more than two acres of land to the Mount Hope community. It is a little unusual to find a church and a cemetery side by side in this region. This date places these important community features at an early time in the settlement period. It is a special credit to this little community that the church is still prized and cared for and that the cemetery, with its superb view of the area, is so well kept and is still the site of burials for so many community citizens.

A regular Memorial Day observance with a program that brings throngs of people to the little church has been a tradition. This

(Photo from the Mount Hope Community History).

long standing rite has brought Mount Hope a notable degree of prestige in the ranks of pioneer communities.

Lone Pine—about four miles west of Tekoa. It was an important early-day way stop on the way into the north Palouse. It predated Tekoa, but was quickly pushed into decline when the railroad went that way.

In explaining the community name, local history relates that a single pine tree on a hilltop had a role as a landmark on the stage route heading north from Farmington. Here a big log building was erected to serve as a combination stage depot, post office, store and briefly, as a schoolhouse. The location of these facilities became known as "Lone Pine."

A local poet soon penned a set of verses to commemorate the sentinel tree.

>I have seen lots of trees that were planted
>In straight and orderly line,
>But I have never seen a tree
>That could rival that old friend of mine.
>It is only a pine tree, you murmur,
>Only a lone, lone pine,
>But a childhood dreams, it still holds it seems,
>A place in this heart of mine.
>
>Old pine tree, you may be lonely,
>Standing alone on the hill,
>But you were put there for a purpose;
>I'm sure it was God's will,
>To place you there in the grainfield
>To guard as the soldier must
>The children who grew up around you,
>So in God we would put our trust.

The Clark Family Story and Lone Pine

Family biographies like that of Mrs. I. N. Clark are often one of the few remaining connections to old communities like Lone Pine. This story is edited from the Tekoa Community History (1962). Some individuals have a special gift for relating interesting and informative stories. Mrs. Lucy Clark's account is a good depository of pioneer lore—particularly the now rare details about the Lone Pine area.

Lucy was born in 1851, the seventh of fourteen children born to Jesse and Nancy Dollarhide. She pens an interesting account of her childhood and her family's wagon trek west to the Sacramento Valley. She was only fourteen when she met her husband to be. It was evidently love at first sight and they were quickly married. Her husband was sixteen years her senior. They were married in 1865.

Lucy had an unusual last maiden name, but her new husband had an even more unusual given name. He was Ichabod Niles Clark—all of his life he went by his initials, I.N. (Clark).

In the fall of 1873 the Clarks moved north to the Rouge River Valley in Oregon. Then in 1880, they decided to move further north to Washington Territory where Lucy had a sister. Traveling via Umatilla, Walla Walla, and Colfax, they eventually came to the area between Latah and Tekoa. Lucy made one particularly unusual and interesting comment as they approached their new home, "The road from Colfax was just furrows that had been made with a plow." She added there was only one family in the whole Oakesdale area.

When they arrived they had seventy-five dollars to build a house, live through the winter and prepare to file on a homestead. "It froze early, but we managed to put up a board and batten house, a shed for their livestock and drag in a good pile of tamarack logs for fuel—we got settled in for the winter.

Continuing her story she goes on to say, "There were many good people at Lone Pine." She specifically mentions a Mr. Russel who ran the stage depot-store complex and the fact that he let the early pioneers use a room in his establishment for the first school. Soon a log schoolhouse was built. It later burned to the ground and still another building served as the schoolhouse and a sort of community center and the site for the first church services. Mrs. Clark even tells that the church had a United Brethren affiliation—the first minister was a relative of Lucy's. The beginning of the little community was firmly in place but its existence was to be relatively short-lived.

The Clarks were a popular and a well liked couple and they occupied a prominent place on the local scene. The couple had eleven children. After long, eventful lives they were laid to rest in the Lone Pine Cemetery.

Lone Pine Cemetery

The cemetery today: There are still a few surviving record books for the cemetery. This was a project of a small group of locals in the 1970's, when they gathered all the surviving data that could be found. They reported a total of 115 burials. Only 56 markers could be found. It is possible some graves have been relocated. The last burial was in 1953. It is noted, "This cemetery is no longer used for internments."

This cemetery is at an isolated location today. Moreover, the site is very overgrown with shrubs, rose brush and grass. The cemetery road, alleys and markers are almost indiscernible. Looking for an individual grave site could be a real challenge.

A final note—in the 1970's the little group of locals observed a special feature at the site: "It is about the only acreage in a wide radius where native flowers and shrubs, as well as prairie bunch grass, still may be found in their natural state."

Lone Pine's Obscure Church

The early day church built to the northwest of the Lone Pine community is now an especially little known remnant of area history. It was one of the few regional churches that stood alone in open farm country.

I was really surprised when I saw its designation and location in the 1910 Whitman County Atlas because I had never seen or heard any mention of it that I could remember. Then it came back to me! I had just enough of a memory to go back and read Mrs. Clark's mention of a little United Brethren Church in the Lone Pine community.

I made a few local inquiries that elicited no response at all. Then I also remembered an area resident from an old pioneer family. I knew this person had a vivid interest in pioneer history and she came to the rescue with a number of enlightening details.

Jane Eberle has retired on her family farm and she recalled her grandmother's story of this nearby church. Jane was even able to find a faded photograph. The church was a small, non-descript building; even lacking any sign of the typical church steeple. Except for the positive identification, it could have easily been thought to be a schoolhouse. This church had a relatively short existence. Before long the local people transferred their attendance to the churches in nearby towns.

More Solitary And Secluded Cemeteries

There are several old and historic cemeteries that warrant a mention in a list of obscure places in the region.

The Butte Cemetery—located on the northwest corner of Starr Butte in Rock Creek valley. The older citizens of that area estimated there were as many as seventy-five pioneers buried there. There were also stories of Indian burials at this site. Native Americans and whites were not buried together at very many locations.

The Butte Cemetery had a direct connection to the Bethel Church, which is identified elsewhere in this book as the oldest church in the area. This cemetery was originally on a primary travel route, but later road changes made it an isolated, hard to reach location. Also, by that time the Bethel Church was relocated to Rockford.

Still later in time, many of the graves were moved to other locations and today there are only a few graves remaining. For a long time several local men knew some of the history of family burials and did some yearly clean-up and maintenance. Today a solitary visitor or a person checking on family genealogy would be a rare event.

The Sanders Creek Cemetery—located a few miles southeast of Chapman Lake. This is another "forgotten" burial site. It also has the unusual story of whites and Indians sharing the same final resting place.

Local folklore here tells about Indian deaths from smallpox. One of the oldest locals tells of her youth when children were "warned away" by that story. This was a small burial site with only a few local family internments.

The Riggs Cemetery—the last cemetery to be mentioned is about two miles northeast of Rosalia. The earliest marked grave is that of the son of the town's founder—Willie Whitman, dated 1879. This was a large pioneer cemetery. Research estimates it had as many as one hundred and fifty graves. The Riggs site was on a hilly, rugged road that made access difficult. In 1903 a new cemetery was plotted with easier access and nearer to Rosalia. The majority of burials were quickly diverted to the new cemetery, and eventually a number of graves were moved to the new site.

The Riggs Cemetery became almost forgotten. In a sense of melodrama, some locals called it a lost "City of the Dead." By the 1950's a wide interest had begun surfacing to gather and preserve pioneer history. This was considered to be a good example of a locally important site. Community organizations volunteered to straighten old stones and clear overgrown plots, also records were recovered and preserved. Now the Riggs Cemetery provides a good example of a commitment to our pioneer heritage.

Old Rural Schools

There is one part of history in the realm of old pioneer places that has had an ongoing degree of interest and priority. That subject is the old pioneer schools. The area's historical societies have preserved volumes of school records and pictures of both students and buildings; these materials have been carefully documented and filed. As an example the Southeast Spokane County Historical Society has put together a two-volume set of school histories for their area and they are available for inspection and purchase.

The place of the one-room rural school is one of the most sentimental of all pioneer themes. Today nearly all of these old buildings are gone. One still survives in southeast Spokane County. It has been a favorite subject for this writer.

The Prairie View School

At a location very near the center of the northern Palouse and at an isolated country road junction is a ramshackle relic of one of the most romanticized memories of pioneer history. It is one of the very last examples of the one-room schoolhouse of yesteryear. This old school is at a location about five miles southwest of Waverly, where it operated until 1936.

Today the building's roof is almost gone, the windows are gaping holes and the inside of the building and the floor are a shambles. Amazingly, the frame and the bell tower still stand relatively straight and true, but it is certain that the building's physical condition is very precarious.

Once, rural schools like this were common at about five-mile intervals. This was the distance determined by how far children could walk to school. Some children did ride horseback to school, and a horse barn was a frequent companion building. There might also be a dwelling for the teacher—usually known as the teacher's "cottage," but rather commonly a teacher would "board" with a nearby family.

This school was once a center for a little community. Social events and church services were held there. Now a few old-timers will still fondly reminisce about events at the "Little Red School." (A bright coat of red paint gave it a special distinction in the region's lexicon.)

(Dan Bothell Photo)

I only live a few miles from this old relic. It is at a lonely setting nowadays, but I usually stop several times a year and take a closer look at what the ravages of time are wreaking on this old landmark.

About two years ago while driving by I saw a car in front of the building, and I immediately thought some past area resident was making a nostalgic visit. When I looked inside, I found that the visitors were two teenage girls. They were from north of Spangle and attend the present-day Liberty consolidated school in the area. As we began a brief exchange of comments, I told them that I had attended a similar nearby school in the final closing period of these little schools operating in the late 1930's. As we talked, our eyes brightened, our voices became animated and we seemed to share a special intergenerational experience. That these young ladies felt the attraction and wonder of this old site, was to me, something very special.

Whenever I stop and look into this old building my mind is always flooded with memories. As I get ready to leave, I take a final look at the sagging boards and the gaping door and windows. A last look at the bell tower brings thoughts of the events it overlooked and the people who have passed under its shadow. As I drive away, I always experience a sense of real emotion as I contemplate that part of history will soon pass from the scene, and what memories that are still left will grow dimmer.

In conclusion, there is a large degree of irony and melodrama in a review of "forgotten places." There are almost always stories of interest connected to the old sites and why they for a time flourished, but with a few exceptions, are now often remembered only faintly, if at all.

(Dan Bothell Photo)

Curlew

Prairie Chicken

Vole

Coyote

(Sketch assistance by Evelyn Leitz)

CHAPTER 9

Some Historic Birds And Animals Of The Palouse

Background

Some of the native animals and birds of the Palouse are now gone. The fast and elusive pronghorn antelope was fairly common. Noted for agility and an impetuous curiosity, it still survives in very limited numbers in the desert-like areas of central Washington. And buffalo, in limited numbers, were found in eastern Washington, but by the time the white man arrived, rare bleached skeletons were about all that still existed.

As noted earlier in this book, it is an interesting part of Indian history that when the red man gained access to the horse - only about a hundred years before the arrival of the white man - they quickly made a priority of going east across the Rockies to hunt buffalo. That mobility made a dramatic change in their lifestyle.

Local game animals were never plentiful enough to provide the aboriginal people with very much of their food supply. That fell to the migratory fish runs. In supplementing that primary staple of their diet, their hunting pressure kept the number of deer, elk and antelope at a relatively modest population. When the horse gave the local Indians the opportunity to add an important red meat resource to their diet, they readily undertook the long and difficult trek across the mountains and faced the danger of conflict with the warlike "Buffalo Indians." It made it very clear they were eager for a new food staple and useful hides that could be found to the east.

As the white man began to dominate the Palouse, the larger game animals faced even greater hunting pressure. Deer were scarce, and the larger species—namely elk and moose—became almost unknown. Later as deer hunting became mainly a sporting endeavor, local nimrods traveled to distant mountain areas to find deer hunting. Elk and moose hunting really required distant safaris. Then game animals made some dramatic adjustments.

First, the local deer population climbed to the point where hunting became readily available right here at home. Next, in about the last 25 years elk have become increasingly common and are now a regular part of the Palouse wildlife scene. After all the game biologist commentaries about elk needing roadless and primitive areas, elk are widely seen in the Palouse, especially adjacent to the north and eastern borders. In fact, crop damage has become a large issue and has resulted in special hunting to deal with this problem.

Just recently, moose are becoming more common. These large and dramatic animals are noted for highly unpredictable behavior. If they continue to appear more frequently, it would seem likely that some interesting adjustments will be called for.

With increasing populations of larger game animals occurring, there are now concerns about mountain lions and even wolves that are becoming common topics of debate and discussion. Looking back across history may help provide a useful understanding of these evolving changes.

Historic Fauna of the Palouse Country:

The wildlife of the area in early times provides many interesting topics for consideration. When the first settlers arrived on the scene in the Palouse, wildlife was often an important part of their food supply. No creature was more important than the native bird the pioneers called the "prairie chicken." It is another interesting example of an important part of history that is now almost forgotten.

Prairie chickens were a feature of pioneer life throughout much of the pioneer west. They are members of the grouse family that are particularly well adapted to the grassland prairies—the same prairies that attracted prospective farmers. It was to be ironic that the attraction of these fertile prairies for farming would inevitably seal the fate of these birds.

The sharp-tail grouse is the sub-species name of the birds found locally. The sharp-tail was not a colorful, showy bird like the ring-neck pheasant we see in the area today. In size and appearance it is somewhat similar to the female pheasant. It was related and similar in appearance to some of the grouse species that still survive in ranching country in Montana and some of the other plains states.

These prairie grouse have some unusual and endearing characteristics—one of its most interesting and noticeable habits is its spring mating dance. In its fullest plumage and with neck area wind sacks inflated, the male grouse "struts his stuff" to attract female birds. At dawn these footloose frenzies would begin as the male bird spreads his wings and puffs up the purple neck sacks. Driven by the hormones of the mating cycle he rattles the shafts of his tail feathers in a staccato sound sometimes compared to a miniature jackhammer.

It is little wonder that many of the dance centered rituals and costumes of the plains Native Americans are derived from this part of nature's show and display.

The "dancing ground" where this activity occurs each season has its own special place in the prairie chicken saga. It has its own special name...a lek. Leks usually have less vegetation and are more open than surrounding areas. This allows the birds to see and be seen. Here is where the birds will gather in March and April for this special mating ritual.

Today the sharp-tail's drastic decline in numbers has led to intensive study in the few areas where they still survive. These leks enable biologists to study the scant remnants of the species and monitor their chance of survival.

Once it was observed that flocks of prairie chickens could darken the sky. They had little natural fear of man and though they were fast and elusive in flight they were easily shot in large numbers. It was not this hunting that led to their demise. It was the change of habitat that occurred with settlement. Less cover, less native grass and shrubs that provided their winter diet, and the plowing of the leks—these were to be insurmountable odds. Game biologists last saw these birds in the far south of the Palouse in the 1940's. They ended up at isolated spots like Steptoe Canyon on the breaks of the Snake River. In the late 1800's the sharp-tails were the most abundant bird in the Pacific Northwest. Now the prairie chicken is nearly a forgotten memory in the region's history.

Other Bird Species

Some smaller birds of the Palouse prairies—like the Curlew (see comment as a place name in Rock Creek Valley), also did not easily withstand the onset of farming. The Curlew was a bird with long legs and a long, curved beak. It lived on the borders of wet, low lying regions and along creek banks.

A similar bird that makes its home on the wet borders of the region is the Common Snipe. It has faired well enough to survive in small numbers in the region today. Does nocturnal "Snipe Hunting" still survive among the youth of today? I would suppose it probably does. (Note: Snipe Hunting is a prank involving taking some "initiate" out at night with a sack to catch a snipe!)

Song Birds

The beauty of some of the older species of songbirds is a part of local legend. The vivid flashes of color and the melodic songs of native birds like the Western Bluebird and the American Goldfinch are now far too rare. Still, specialized preservation efforts can show some success. Some bird lovers go all out to make their homes and yards bird friendly. Nesting box projects are preserving some Bluebirds. The Turnbull Refuge southeast of Cheney is stellar example of what extra efforts can achieve, and now draws many visitors to see their Bluebird population.

Farther afield, a surprising piece of good news is that the hybrid poplar plantations in the Columbia Basin are prime Goldfinch habitat.

Special Area Animals

The jackrabbit has disappeared from the Palouse scene. The native jackrabbit is an animal of the prairies and plains. It is an animal of specialized abilities. When it comes to running, it can attain speeds up to forty miles per hour. Jumping, it can achieve a five-yard leap. Highly developed rear legs are a trademark. Long and very large ears are another special feature. They are a main detector device for eluding predators. They also serve an additional function in hot weather and, in warm regions, as an effective tool to dissipate body heat.

Jackrabbits are comparatively solitary, active at night and need a large range per rabbit, especially in drier areas. In earlier times they were actively hunted for sport and to minimize crop damage.

The American Badger is an elusive, burrowing animal with a reputation for an aggressive behavior if it is provoked or threatened. It is a compact, heavily boned and muscled animal. It has long forelimbs and short back legs, both with powerful claws that make it a natural digging machine and a capable fighter. Its main food source is small rodents. With the decline of the ground squirrel population it has become notably less common.

The Columbia Ground Squirrel derives this name from its home in inter-mountain regions of the Columbia Plateau. These ground squirrels survived mainly on grass or grain vegetation, lived in colonies and have an interesting trait in common with their well-known cousins, the prairie dog. They are noted for standing on a mound of dirt at the entrance to their burrows and sounding a shrill alarm if any danger comes near.

With the advent of grain farming, they became a major pest for farmers, up until about the time of World War II. When many of today's seniors were growing up, most farm families gave their children the responsibility of setting a squirrel trap line in the spring season. It was one of the rites of farm childhood.

Squirrels lived along field borders and roads where the fences of that time kept areas protected with a cover of grass and shrubs where the squirrels would have cover. When the crops began to emerge and grow, these pests could make huge inroads, and the crop loss was a major problem. Poisoning was another control measure, and almost every farm boy would have a .22 rifle for squirrel hunting. This was also a "macho" rite of spring.

None of these measures were as successful as the farmers would have wished, but at last diseases became a major factor, and squirrel populations dropped dramatically. At times the squirrel populations would seem to recover a bit, but then disease and predators would again seem to reduce them to small numbers. Now the times of squirrel trap lines and squirrel poisoning are only a distant memory.

The Meadow Vole (Mouse) is a native rodent species that is only rarely seen, but its presence can be a big concern to Palouse farmers at any time. It is now probably one of the most common animal species in the Palouse. It has a population cycle that varies dramatically with the weather and natural events. In optimum conditions it has always been a serious pest in grain fields. This little rodent is one of the primary food sources for one of the real standouts of the Palouse animal family.

The ornery, mischievous Coyote now comes to the spotlight. This is one native animal had readily survived the transition in the Palouse from prairie to farmland, and in fact, it has thrived. Originally only commonly found in the far west, the coyote has now spread over much of the North American continent. In bygone days predators like wolves and bears, and competition for food, kept the numbers and the range of the coyotes well in check. Today their main enemy is man, but despite humans' best efforts, man's presence doesn't seem a dominant factor in the saga of this "varmint."

In early settlement times when the Palouse had a significant livestock population, farm flocks of sheep were common. Sheep and coyotes make a poor combination, and coyotes were hunted extensively. Government trappers were brought in to reduce the animals' numbers with both poison and traps. This had only a limited success.

After World War II, local veterans took up flying in a big way. Almost every community would have at least one flying club. Hunting coyotes by airplanes became a popular wintertime "sport." Airplanes were usually fitted with skis, and doors or windows provided access for rifles or shotguns. A regular air militia was in vogue. The flying club scene has pretty much faded away. Now snowmobiles provide the major focus for winter hunting. Still the coyote readily survives.

Weather factors and food supplies are more of a determinant in the numbers than any of man's puny efforts. Coyotes can eat about anything. Mice, squirrels and other rodents have, in general, followed farming to become plentiful. Then add tidbits like grasshoppers, frogs, fish, snakes, fruit and vegetables, carrion, birds...house cats...the list goes on!

The coyote is intelligent, wily and amazingly adaptable to every situation. They have a capacity for playfulness and independence. The fact that they can be so bothersome and obnoxious only makes them more of an item of attention and notoriety. The yipping song of the coyote, long a feature and trademark of western lore, seems destined to be here a long time.

One other feature of the coyote's story should be mentioned—the coyote had a very important place in Indian legend and mythology. The combination of intelligence, mischievousness and other traits just referred to gave him a dominant role among the animal people in the creation stories about the time before humans existed. Now, after eons of time, the coyote is still a dominant symbol and icon, both of the past and the west of today.

Aquatic Animals

The attraction of the fur trade was one of the major focuses of the white man in earliest times in the region. The Palouse prairies were not particularly notable in this regard, but they did have a modest population of beavers and other fur bearers along regional streams. These animals soon came close to extinction, but natural cycles have repeated, and today beavers, muskrats and even an occasional rarer species can still be seen.

I vividly remember when I was a local student in the World War II years when government trappers came to the Latah area to catch beavers to transplant to other regions. The interesting part of this event was that most of the local people seemed unaware that Hangman Creek had again become beaver habitat and even had a trappable surplus.

In recent times beavers are still present. Their numbers seem to vary greatly and be closely related to food supplies. Other species seem to follow the same cyclical patterns. Another item of great interest has been the appearance of river (fresh water) otters. Their population is limited, and their appearance is erratic. They appear to be migratory in pursuit of their food supply. They are certainly an amazing addition to the local wildlife scene.

Note: Spangle pioneer William Hart provided an interesting final look at the place original game species occupied in the pioneer era Palouse, saying, "The family rifle or shotgun was an important means of keeping the family larder stocked with food. My dad took up a place not far from Spangle. We had no stove, just a fireplace, and I remember he would frequently melt bullets for his old muzzleloader—the source of most of our meat supply.

"The Palouse country was alive with game such as curlew, sage hen and prairie chicken. Then, the potholes and creeks were frequented by ducks, geese and cranes, and the ravines and wooded hills had deer and blue grouse. If you were lucky you might even be able to sell some venison for six or eight cents a pound and prairie chickens for around a dollar for a dozen."

CHAPTER 10

Old Newspaper Stories

A Window to the Past

To look through old area newspapers is a special way to get a sense of pioneer life. The events of interest from the newspapers of that era are somewhat similar to what we read today, except that it had a much wider scope. People did not have all the access to what we now know as an almost smothering media. They depended solely on the newspapers to cover the entire gamut of what made the world and the society of that day tick, and often it was described as a somewhat florid style that had its own particular dialect and color.

The newspapers were the only window on the more distant world but then, as now, the local scene was the big focus, so the newspapers highlighted local events of every description. Parties, dances and social events were always covered. Fraternal orders and lodges outlined their meetings and activities. Speakers, literary societies, church events, school events and just plain neighborly visiting, all were covered. A popular column of that day would be a gossipy column, "Around the Town," which would tell the doings and foibles of the prominent and not so prominent.

Other regular stories would highlight crime and law enforcement and the "appearances" before the local Justice of the Peace or a nearby court judge. Fires, accidents, etc., were frequent occurrences. (Fires were often a major disaster because of primitive fire control measures.)

The range of subject matter went on to more domestic topics. Articles on homemaking tips, health hints, poetry, book reviews and often weekly installments of fictional stories were printed. Certainly cartoon features and jokes and humor were popular and, as always, the local sports events had a huge appeal.

The greater number of people in the Palouse and the large number of businesses to supply local needs made advertising a particularly thriving part of the local newspaper business. When we see the modest prices advertised in those times, we usually do rather dramatic double takes! Finally, birth and death announcements and legal notices would be the wrap up—much like today. In every sense, the newspapers did it all!

The newspapers reviewed most intensively for this section were first, the *Rosalia Citizen* in about the period from 1904 to 1909. Special thanks go to Rosalia historian Erma Jean Widman, who researched and published a recent (2004) booklet of historic news stories from that paper. It warrants mention that the Citizen regularly printed news from an area as large as from Cheney to St. John and Colfax, and from Rockford to Tekoa on the east. A second main source of stories was the *Fairfield*

Standard. Like all papers of that era, it went through a number of name changes and reincarnations. It was a direct ancestor or parent of the area's present-day weekly newspaper, *North Palouse Journal*.

Of Local Interest

Bad Runaway

Tuesday afternoon, the dray team of L. Long's transfer house was standing on Whitman Street (Rosalia) when the horses became frightened and started down the street on their own account and at a speed greatly in excess of the speed limit. The dray was piled high with furniture and household goods belonging to Peter Sundin, and the way furniture was scattered along the street was a caution. The team turned down Seventh Street and across the tracks and finally ran against a post on the west side and was stopped. The load of furniture was badly smashed and a great deal of it will be a complete loss.

Factory Stops for Beets

(October 1905) The sugar factory was obliged to stop operations last Tuesday morning on account of the scarcity of beets. The continued bad weather has made the beet harvest very backward, and the supply could not keep pace with the factory consumption. This season has been an unfortunate one all around for the beet grower, but the combinations of bad circumstances cannot keep up forever.

•••

(June 1907) The first Canada Thistle (one of today's most pernicious noxious weeds) in the vicinity has been found growing along the O.R.&N. right of way.

Fish for the Lakes

(May 1907) The fish to stock Rock Lake and Bonnie Lake arrived this morning at Rosalia in charge of a special messenger from Fisheries Station, Oregon City, Oregon. The fish were taken to the lakes today.

The stocking of Rock Lake and Bonnie was secured through an effort of the Rosalia Hyak Club and under the club's management the fish were transferred to the lakes. The consignment consists of land-locked salmon for Rock Lake and eastern brook trout for Bonnie Lake. These species were placed in the lake at the recommendation of U.S. Commissioner Bowers, under whose direction the fish were delivered at Rosalia.

The number of each of the species sent was about 5,000 for each lake, all of them about an inch and a half long. The belief is that the natives of the lakes to which the fish have been assigned are well adapted to the propagation of the species, and the local anglers are anticipating great sport at the lakes in the not distant future.

•••

A ten-year-old lad named Miller, living south of Cheney, struck a dynamite cap with a hammer. Dr. Turner amputated some of his fingers and will bring him through if blood poisoning lets him alone.

•••

Enjoying a 'Libation'

Two of the three saloons doing business in Fairfield have closed their doors, for the time being, on account of the $1,000 license imposed by the council. J. E. Modrell's license expired on the 9th and Fred Miller's on the 12th, and both proprietors promptly closed their places of business. D. F. Spurgin's license does not run out until October 18th. If the saloon men stand pat in their determination not to take out licenses at the $1,000 figure, Fairfield will likely be dry during the life of the present council.

A Later Follow-up

(September 21, 1906) That whosoever thirsteth for a drink of wet goods may assuage his thirst in Fairfield is now an assured fact. Last Friday afternoon J. E. Modrell deposited a $1,000 check and took out a saloon license for one year...

***

Fairfield, Washington

(June 2, 1908) A youthful embryo steeplejack struck terror into the hearts of a few citizens last Tuesday night who happened to look toward the tower of the water tank. A small boy was balanced on the top of the tank with arms outstretched, proud monarch of all he surveyed. Fortunately, the lad's equilibrium was perfect; otherwise, it would have been a different story.

Look for Big Wages

(June 1906) Already there are hundreds of men looking for employment with the farmers of Washington, the heavy advance guard having arrived in the southern part of the state.

It is stated there seems to be an inclination among these men to demand a little more than the established wages. The situation is apparently leading them to believe they can enforce their demands. The fixed pay is $5 per day, but some of the workmen, claiming to be first class, said they won't work for less than $7 and refused offers of $6. The farmers are willing to pay liberal wages for capable help but do not have the slightest notion of standing for holdups. The situation, however, is serious. Efforts are now being made in parts of Whitman County to engage threshing machine crews and other farm laborers are not meeting with the best success.

With the price of grain sacks out of sight and labor demanding exorbitant wage, the skies are not altogether blue, but the Palouse farmer bears himself serenely and does not give way to undue worry. The demand for labor in eastern Washington was never greater. Railway construction has called on most of the help, and contractors are fearful lest farmers will put wages so high their camps will be robbed of men.

Had Bad Lamps

"Say, look here, those horses I bought of you last week are blind—blind as a bat. Why didn't you tell me that before I bought them?"

"I did tell you that, and you said it would be all right."

"When did you tell me that?"

"The day you bought them. Didn't I tell you that they didn't look very good?"

Hoboes are Numerous

The wheat fields are beginning to wave with every breeze, and the "hoboes" are responding to the waving heads as if their motion was that of a beckoning magician's wand.

Harvest time in the Palouse always draws many of the unemployed from other sections that are not as highly favored by the bountiful hand of nature as the rolling Palouse hills. Many of these have some certain point that they visit annually and help in the harvesting of the crops. These are the laboring men who come to the land of plenty to earn an honest dollar.

But there is a large number of real hoboes who consider labor a worse crime than any of the laws man has seen fit to punish. These follow up the men who toil in the fields and employ their time by devising means whereby they eke out an existence without labor.

It is difficult to distinguish between the laborer who is sometimes known as a "blanket stiff" and the real "boe" who abhors work with far more consistence than the average Christian abhors the tempting ruler of the sulfurous pit.

The great activity in railroad building in this section of the state, the crop prospects and the big fair on the coast has helped to draw many of this class west, and as a result there are many of this class drifting into the Palouse towns.

Along the bank of Pine Creek is a favorite resort for the hoboes. Carrying a blanket is too much like work, so they camp beneath the willows and, with a newspaper for a blanket, they put in the night.

Strange as it may seem, many of the hoboes have a fairly good education, and some of them have college degrees. The popular supposition is that the hobo is not equipped mentally for the struggle of life, but this is a great mistake, for it is plain to be seen that any man who can live without an income and without labor must be a clever rascal and not to be trusted.

The Local Crime Scene

Stolen

Myrtle Tipton, a fifteen-year-old girl, stole three horses and a wagon from an Indian on the reservation near Tekoa and sold them for $225 at St. John. She is still at large and presumably dressed in a man's attire.

(Follow-up story several months later) Myrtle Tipton, a girl who stole horses and got into the penitentiary at Walla Walla last fall, is having troubles all her own. She accidentally swallowed a pin one day last week, and an operation on her throat was necessary for its removal.

(Articles like this were very common. Reports of an event were followed up with a current report to bring the reader up to date.)

•••

It is reported from Endicott that City Marshall____ _____ gave Councilman _____ _____ a good larruping* because the latter was too willing to run the marshal's office and "rubbed it into him till he couldn't stand it any longer."

Larruping is an old-time word describing "a good beating."

•••

New Wagon

Tekoa has a novel "hurry up" wagon. Marshal Dickinson arrested an Indian, Tom Prosper, who was intoxicated and being unable to make the Siwash walk to jail hauled him there in a wheel barrow.

•••

One Indian near Tekoa stole a horse from another Indian, one Tommy Yell. Evidently Tommy yelled, for the thief was arrested and lodged in jail.

•••

(Name omitted), a 14-year-old girl living near St. John, whose mother is dead and whose father's location is unknown, has been pronounced incorrigible and committed to the state Reform School.

•••

A gypsy traveling through town Tuesday traded a broken winded horse to a young son of Mr. McRae for a much better animal. The father overhauled the gypsy and demanded that he "deliver," which he did and hiked back on his own.

•••

Cost Him $8.00

J. Knagge bought a jug Wednesday and was summoned before Judge West and asked to show cause why he should not be fined for being drunk and disorderly. Knagge was not in a position to make any denial and $8.00 and costs closed the incident.

Women Leave Town

(From Tekoa, Washington) As a result of the recent movement against vice, all the disorderly women have left town.

A Bloody Night at Rockford

Rockford had a strenuous Fourth. The trouble began with a dispute over a livery bill. A fierce fight ensued. Fisticuffs and the use of knives followed, with much blood spilt. An alarm followed, and a 25-man posse was sent out to apprehend the main perpetrators. This led to a major gunfight with frightful injuries. Some of the perpetrators of this big melee are still at large!

At St. John

A man was arrested the other night and fined six dollars and costs for using foul language in the streets. It might be well to pass some of that medicine along to sundry other towns.

Gypsies at Fairfield

Gypsies visited this place Wednesday and began their usual program of begging, fortune telling, etc. At a local home one of the women took a new pair of shoes and a blanket, pretending that she understood they were to be given to her. Marshal Gerling was notified, and he shooed the whole outfit on their way. A hot bath in soapy water would be the proper penalty to place on this band of strollers by every town they visit. The need is great.

Youngsters

Those smart youngsters who are silvering over cent pieces and passing them off for dimes, even in a joke, are in a dangerous business. There is a very drastic law against defacing or changing Uncle Sam's coins.

The Electric Railroad

(June 1905) During the past three weeks there has been a dearth of news regarding the probable route of the Spokane & Inland Electric road through the Palouse country. A discreet silence has been maintained by the promoters regarding the matter, and the rumors flying in the air have been only conjecture.

It is now an apparently settled fact, however, that the route will follow the original survey between Mount Hope and Waverly, and the best that Fairfield can hope for is a spur...

(September 1905) The contractors who are grading the Spokane & Inland Electric road report that they have fully 800 men at work. The road is well advanced to a point 20 miles from Spokane, and it is expected to have the road completed as far as Waverly by January 1.

(January 1907) The trolley car whizzed along the streets of Rosalia for the first time last Wednesday evening, and the honking of the horn and the clanging of the bell drew out quite a number of citizens who examined, discussed and offered information.

The trial run was made after night—the car arriving in Rosalia at 8:15. The speed maintained was about eighteen miles per hour. The engines have motors capable of developing 450 horsepower and are attracting considerable interest.

A regular passenger schedule between Spokane and Rosalia is being worked out to go into effect soon.

(April 1907) The proposition to build a branch of the Spokane & Inland Electric railroad from the main line at West Fairfield to Chatcolet on Lake Coeur d'Alene is beginning to assume definite shape. A committee...appointed by the Fairfield Commercial Club for the purpose of interviewing the farmers along the proposed route regarding right of way performed the duty assigned to them Monday and met with flattering encouragement...

(Another note) An Irishman working on the Spokane & Inland near Colfax stole a suit of clothes from a fellow laborer. The latter gave him a terrific thrashing and then took him to jail.

Courting

(1909) Edwin Imhoff, while buggy riding Sunday, ran against a telephone pole and was thrown over a barbed wire fence, breaking his collarbone. The young lady accompanying him was thrown out but was unharmed. The buggy was a total wreck.

A Quick and Safe Remedy of Bowel Complaints

Twenty years ago Mr. Geo. W. Brock discovered that Chamberlain's Colic, Cholera and Diarrhea Remedy was a quick and safe cure for bowel complaints. "During all of these years," he says, "I have used it and recommended it many times, and the results have never yet disappointed me." You can buy your supply at Hardesty's drug store.

Not the Wild West

F. Edwards and A. Spence mixed the "potations" Tuesday afternoon and engaged in the work of giving a "wild west" performance on the street. But when they tried to startle the natives by riding fast and expressed a determination to take their horses into the saloon for a drink, they encountered Marshal Ellis. Edwards, who it is said was the chief promoter of the Wild West entertainment, was introduced to Judge West Tuesday evening and assessed $10.00 and costs. Spence was assessed $5.00 and costs at Wednesday morning's session. The assessments were paid, and Edwards and Spence departed on their way rejoicing.

Notes from Plaza

The members of Plaza Rural Telephone Association assembled Saturday and organized "The Plaza Telephone Company," with ten shareholders, each to hold an equal interest. A committee was appointed to procure 35 poles with wire and insulators; by-laws were adopted and two applications received to join the line.

Some Odds and Ends

(1908 Rockford News) A major controversy has emerged between opposing factions of teachers and patrons at the Rockford School. At issue is the suitability of a number of current literary works. Primary examples cited are the Tom Sawyer and Huckleberry Finn books by Mark Twain. The arguments center around the interest they generate in reading versus the morality of the subject matter. The opposing viewpoints are quite evenly divided, and the resolution of this debate is still up in the air.

(August, 1918) At last the Standard has been able to locate the resting place of the mastodon skeleton mentioned last week. Mr. Nye, Inland railway agent at Waverly, says that he remembers when the other skeleton was dug up and sent east. Ben Coplen, the founder of Latah, was the man who unearthed the bones and started east with them but stopped in Montana and disposed of them to another party who took them to Chicago and sold them to the Field Columbian Museum in that city where they are today. The skeleton is considered the most perfect specimen of a mastodon every discovered in North America. Mr. Coplen always claimed that he knew where another one was located and intended to excavate it, but death intervened.

The location of the skeleton is in a marshy spot along the right of way of the O.W.R. & N., between Fairfield and Latah, along the bank of Hangman Creek. The bones will be taken up and mounted and put in the Spokane museum by the Spokane Historical Society.

Note: This article has several inaccuracies. Although a name commonly used by the public, a mastodon is a smaller and more primitive animal than the Columbia mammoths that made this region famous. Mastodons did live in the Inland Northwest, but very few skeletal remains have been found. Obviously, no skeleton was ever mounted into a local display.

Flu Epidemic Takes Four

(December, 1918) Local situation is improving after a short period of sharp anxiety.

The influenza hospital at the schoolhouse has admitted fourteen patients since opening last Thursday. They have discharged two and lost one by death; the remaining eleven are all progressing nicely.

The citizens have responded freely to the call for donations of bedding, and other articles such as milk, eggs, lemons and oranges are being liberally supplied the sick ones. The four who have fallen victim to the epidemic are all local Fairfield residents.

Seed Peas Shipped

(1906) A carload of seed peas was shipped from Tekoa last week. This was the first car of seed peas ever shipped in Whitman County.

The Police Docket

"Two-Gun Hart" - James Capone

From the *Tekoa Sentinel:* Many residents of Tekoa were amazed last weekend when it was disclosed that Richard J. Hart, former well known figure in Tekoa and nearby Idaho towns on the Coeur d'Alene Indian Reservation, was in reality the long-lost brother of the late gang overlord, Al Capone.

"Two Gun Hart" was identified as James Capone during an income tax investigation in Chicago last week. James Capone, or "Two Gun Hart," as he was known in Tekoa, is now a 63-year-old justice of peace at Homer, Nebraska. He spent four or five years in the Tekoa area in the late 1920s and early 1930s, working closely with Inland Empire police departments, especially the famous "dry squad" of the Spokane prohibition days.

According to the Tekoa Sentinel, there was some disagreement as to how good a shot he was with a gun, but all agreed that he was a good law enforcement officer. He wasn't a big man, but he was wiry and strong. Another veteran plain-clothes man of Spokane said Hart had a "steely eye. He would glare at some Indian he wanted information from, and the fellow would literally wilt under his gaze."

According to the late Paschal J. George, who was at one time Chairman of the Coeur d'Alene Tribal Council, Hart caused a lot of trouble on the Reservation. He was well known in towns around the Reservation.

He is now appearing before a Federal grand jury in Chicago, which is investigating income taxes of another brother, Ralph Capone. He (Two gun Hart) told Chicago reporters he had been a law enforcement officer most of his life. He said he hasn't used the Capone name since leaving Brooklyn, New York, in 1905 when he came west "looking for adventure."

Cataracts have nearly deprived him of sight, and he uses a white cane. Now a justice of peace in Homer Nebraska, he was town marshal there after leaving the Indian service. He lived in Nebraska before he came here (Tekoa) as an Indian agent, returning to Homer after retirement from the service in the Dakotas.

Murder at Latah

(July 1905) G. Hohama, a Japanese, shot and killed Mamie Takakai, eldest daughter of J. Takakai, at the home of the later this morning at 2:30 o'clock and then killed himself by cutting his throat with a razor.

Hohama was an employee at the Takakai home and has been living there for the past three years. During that time he formed an attachment for Miss Takakai.

Yesterday evening Mr. Takakai, father of the girl, and Hohama drove to Waverly to look over some beet fields, and during their absence and up to 10 o'clock last night Miss Takakai entertained another young Japanese, Fred Cokjoka, who is employed as time-keeper in the local Japanese camp.

A friend of Hohama who was here last night went to Waverly and told Hohama that Miss Takakai and Cokjoka were together. Hohama came home and was admitted to the house at 12:30 this morning by Mrs. Takakai.

What happened then, as told by Mrs. Takakai, is as follows: "Hohama came to the door and said he had heard that Mamie and Cokjoka were together during the evening, and it worried him, so he came home... He told me that he knew she had been with him until 10 o'clock. I did not know how he could know that but feared that he had been hiding somewhere and had seen her. Hohama had always loved Mamie since he first came to our house and has repeatedly sought her hand.

"She had promised to be his wife when she was 18 years old, and we have only been trying to keep his mind on that alone and to let her finish her education.

After letting him in, I went to bed and to sleep. The next thing I knew was being awakened by a shot, and I ran into Mamie's room where the shot came from. I found the bed clothes on fire and Mamie wounded. I only heard one shot and did not know that Hohama had a weapon and thought he had used a rifle kept in the house."

Hohama, upon gaining admittance to the house, went to his room and after writing a note...stole upstairs and discharged the five shots of a .32 caliber revolver into her person... He then ran downstairs and into his own room, where he cut his throat with a razor, lay down on the bed and died.

...Miss Mamie Takakai was only 13 years old. She was born in America and was a thoroughly Americanized young lady. She attended school here and was in the seventh grade and was a great favorite with her classmates.

Her father, J. Takakai, is a Japanese labor contractor and has charge of all the Japanese labor employed in the beet fields in this section. He had not returned from Waverly at an early hour this morning.

Jealousy is the only motive for the crime which was committed as the result of the friendly relations between Fred Cokjoka and Miss Takakai. It is rumored that he (Hohama) had threatened her life at different times, but no confirmation can be had as to this.

Pioneer Social Events

In spite of the hard work and limitations imposed by pioneer life, recreation and socializing were still a big priority. At first, social events were very limited. We saw in the very earliest times neighbors might come together with focus of a special meal and dancing to mark a special occasion, like a Christmas observance. A sense of community was an important asset to make a success of pioneer life.

Soon schools and churches began to provide avenues of social and community life. As communities and towns evolved, full-grown fraternal and common interest groups appeared on the scene. Socializing still occurred relatively close to home, but that in no way lessened its importance; in fact, it seemed to enhance it. By the time the area was fully settled, the range of social events was surprising. The examples that follow highlight some of these celebrations.

From the Fairfield Standard:

A picnic and annual meeting will be held at Dau's Grove three miles south of Fairfield on Hangman Creek. The affair has been designated as a "Dutch-Democratic (German) picnic.[1] This, when interpreted, probably means no water will be served on the grounds, but the beer will flow freely.

A follow-up article noted: A large crowd attended the German picnic held at Dau's Grove this past Tuesday. People came from far and near to participate in the gayeties of this annual event.

Fortunately, there were no disagreeable incidents connected with the affair. The crowd was in good humor, and no one showed any disposition to disturb the peace.

Owing to the heavy expense connected with the affair, the net proceeds amounted to only $35.00. This will be used to fit up the pavilion.[2]

> [1] There was a very large German immigrant population in this part of the northern Palouse. Rural fire insurance was either non-obtainable or very expensive, so this ethnic group of pioneers formed their own insurance cooperative or mutual fire insurance company in the 1890s. The ability to speak, read and write German was a requirement, as all business was conducted in German. This requirement was removed at the time of World War I. This company is still in operation today and is the oldest insurance company of this type in the State.
>
> In the early 1900s their annual meetings were combined with a summer picnic. Hundreds of people would attend. On one or two occasions, members and friends from the Spokane area even chartered a train from Spokane to Waverly in order to attend this function. These events had another claim to fame. For 50 cents you could have unlimited access to barrels of beer. [Rowdies and troublemakers abused this practice, and it was rather quickly, but sadly, abandoned.]
>
> [2] A pavilion was a structure designed for either a picnic area or community or town gatherings. It could be just a raised wooden floor for dancing in the open, or it might have a roof for shade and shelter. In towns it could be a full-fledged building used the "year 'round" for entertainment, sporting events and anything else in the way of a community event.

German Picnic (Courtesy of Albert Schmitz Family)

Waverly Pavilion from "A History of Waverly"

Old Settlers' Picnics

A special feature of community life in the early 1900s was the "Old Settlers' Picnic." These picnics have now become almost forgotten, but they were an unusually interesting part of history.

The pioneers who together had shared the unique experiences of that time and age found a common bond in these events as they became the seniors and the older generation. One of their great joys would be to gather together and share the laughter, the tears and the memories of those eventful times. They formed a brother- and sisterhood that had few equals in shared experiences.

This reservoir of first-hand experience passed on. Fortunately, the stories that the younger members of the community heard at these events were one of the focuses to preserve the stories of the pioneers in this area.

From The Rosalia Citizen

(July 1, 1904) Headline: Old Settlers' annual picnic and reunion at Fry's Grove—three miles north of Rosalia on Saturday, July 16.

This report tells of plans for the coming celebration to be held at Fry's Grove. It will be the observance of the one-hundred-and-twenty-eighth anniversary of the nation's birth and promises as much enthusiasm as ever. The committee in charge states that arrangements are nearing completion, and visitors can expect a day of pleasure. Everyone is invited to come and bring their basket lunch to spend the day in the grove.

The planned program is to start at 9:30 in the morning and will go all day. Music, speaking, band selections, climbing the greased pole, games, races and a 40X140 pavilion for dancing in the afternoon and evening. (This was a huge dance floor.) There were fireworks in the evening, "buses" to run to and from the grounds. Firecrackers, flags, refreshments and fireworks will be sold on the grounds.

The organization has members at Oakesdale, Tekoa, Latah, Rosalia, Spangle, Waverly, Plaza, Pine City, Thornton, Cheney and St. John. This year's celebration promises to be the biggest ever.

•••

(July 15, 1904) Over two thousand people are expected to gather on the old battle ground at North Pine and put in the day renewing old acquaintances and talking over the days of "auld lang syne." All the old timers who have not yet been called to cross the great divide are looking forward to the day with much pleasure. They will meet their old friends of a quarter of a century ago, and many of the interesting, historic, humorous incidents of pioneer days will be recalled from the fading memories of the past and discussed anew. The Old Settlers' reunions are proving a source of pleasure to both old and young. The main oration of the day is expected to be by Judge S. J. Chadwick of Colfax. The Rosalia School Athletics baseball team will play Spring Valley at Fry's Grove tomorrow.

•••

(July 22, 1904) Fully 2000 people were present at the Old Settlers' picnic and reunion held in Fry's Grove Saturday. The day was an ideal one for an outing, as the rain of the day before laid the dust and freshened the air. The old settlers within a radius of twenty miles were there and indulged in reminiscent tales of the early days when cities in the Inland Empire were not and the howling coyote whined his melancholic cry on every hill and valley. These reminiscences recalled many an ancient incident and renewed many an olden tie which had been broken by the advent of railroads and the accompanying bustle of business and development of the agricultural industry.

The lengthy program of speeches, music and songs was well rendered. Judge L. B. Nash of Spokane was the chief orator (Judge Chadwick of Colfax must have demitted) and delivered an eloquent address woven from the incidents and achievements of a quarter of a century ago.

The grove is located at or near the point where the Indians made their first

Note: This location has now become known as North Pine. It is an intersection for a number of area roads. It had a good-sized rural school in early times. It was also a "flag stop" location of the Northern Pacific Railroad.

attack in the memorable battle with Col. Steptoe and had any survivors of that day chanced to pass the numbers gathered on the historic place it would have been sufficient proof that the hardships and privations were not in vain and that many share the opulent legacy.

Settlers' Picnic at Smythe's Ford

The historic Smythe's Ford site on Hangman Creek was another location with an interesting connection to the subject of old settlers' picnics. The ford on Hangman Creek had become an increasingly isolated site as time went by, and the newer roads bypassed this area, but its location still had a good deal of interest and sentiment to the older pioneers. Also, it was at a central location for a large area, so the region's old-timers decided to buy a 40-acre parcel as a location for an annual meeting and picnic site. Here their annual get-together was a big feature of local community life in the early decades of the 1900s.

This specific location has now almost become forgotten, but the 1912 Spokane County Atlas comes to the rescue and pinpoints this tract of land just west of the "hanging site" monument and across the creek. Here there was ample room for the activities and entertainment that would make up a full day of programs and activities.

When it was decided to erect the monument at this historic location in the mid-1930s, the settlers' association was one of the sponsoring groups. Another relic of that era at this location was the "hanging tree" itself. For many years a prominent local farmer was the president of the settlers' group. He would make it a personal project each year to point out the hanging tree to any newcomers. Each year he would delight in pointing out a different tree as the exact spot where the grizzly hangings had occurred—always with a sly smile that seemed to highlight an unusual and wry sense of humor!

Last Days of the Settlers' Picnic

As the surviving pioneers became fewer and fewer, they moved their get-together to Spokane. The thinning ranks of the survivors merited more attention by the public, and their memories and reminiscences became increasingly noticed.

Eventually the somber day arrived when the last pioneer was laid to rest. Like the loss of a very rare and very special memento, an important connection to past events was gone.

CHAPTER 11

Local Pioneer Stories

Palouse Mammoth Finds - The Coplens and the Donahoes

Mammoths were an exotic, elephant-like creature that roamed the earth over a period of hundreds of thousands of years. The huge animals dominated our area some 10,000 years ago, after the last ice age ended.

The geography of this region was basically the same then as it is today, but the temperature was colder and a strange assortment of animals lived here: primitive horses and camels, huge beavers, and giant sloths; immense wolves, bears, and saber-toothed cats; large primitive deer, elk, and bison. All trod the vast prairies and forests, making what must have been a mind-boggling menagerie.

The mammoths were especially notable for a number of reasons. They needed huge amounts of food to maintain their sheer bulk. Continuing climate changes made variations in their food supply that appeared to be the primary factor in their demise. Some sources would like to claim that hunting by the aboriginal people was a major cause for their disappearance, but now that view is generally given little credit.

Seemingly, the springs and bogs that occurred in the area could "crust over" in the drier season and this could result in death traps for the mammoths when they ventured onto these sites. This would explain the large bone caches that would later prove to be so dramatic.

A "follow up dig" near Latah just prior to 1920. (Photo from the Eastern Washington Historical Society)

112

Shortly after the first settlers arrived, and almost before they were settled into a regular routine of life, some of the more inquisitive ones began to eye the murky springs and bogs that formed part of the local geography. The strange objects in the murk seemed to deserve attention and soon men were grappling into the depths with long poles and iron hooks.

In 1876, along Hangman Creek near Latah, members of the pioneer Coplen family were the first to uncover a major find. Their site yielded a huge assortment of bones and tusks, creating a pandemonium of interest and attention. Soon all of the region's springs were being probed and searched. Traces of a variety of pre-historic animals were found, but generally in rather limited quantities.

Then a few months later, there was another important find twelve miles away on Pine Creek, just southeast of Rosalia. Here two brothers, Bill and Tom Donahoe, had begun probing their site when they hooked onto a submerged object that required a major effort to retrieve! They pulled and heaved with all their combined strength but couldn't budge whatever it was that their grapple had connected with. They rigged up a complex set of tripods and pulleys, but this also proved to be ineffectual.

As many as eight or nine neighbors were recruited to supply additional manpower. Even a drainage ditch was dug to aid the extraction. Finally, perseverance bore fruit and a huge skull was wrestled from the muck. Even though the tusks had been torn off in the struggle, the skull was an eye-popping three-plus feet in width!

A large assortment of thighs, pelvises, backbones and other assorted skeleton remains were found at both the aforementioned locations. To some people's dismay, the huge sweeping tusks that were the trademark feature of the mammoth were soft and brittle and many fell apart on exposure to air.

The Coplen site was the winner in sheer number and weight of bones recovered. Other sites continued to be investigated, though with far less success. Both finders of the major bone stashes loaded up an assortment of their mammoth bones and "went on tour" through much of the Northwest, with plans to even go as far as San Francisco. However, the farmers' taste for show business turned cold. They sold their specimens, which ended up in the possession of scientific organizations in the East.

Palouse area mammoth finds received world wide attention. Widely noted paleontologists were fascinated with this story and several prominent scientists came and made serious efforts to uncover their own finds. However, they had no real degree of success in their searches. The bones from the Latah find were the basis for a major display at a pre-1900 Chicago Exposition (a forerunner of today's World Fairs). At the conclusion of the Exposition, they were put into the Field Museum at Chicago, where they are still part of an important display. The huge Pine Creek skull is at the American Museum of Natural History in New York.

Our region's "Mammoth Finds" have a real claim to fame in contributing to this important story of history and science. Numerous specimens of post-ice age animal remains have continued to be uncovered in area river banks, road cuts and shallow lakes, but nothing has ever quite equaled these local events of the 1870's.

Joe Henry—A North Palouse Historical Icon

(Photo from the Southeast Spokane County Historical Society)

Few historical commentaries for this area fail to mention Joe Henry the famed mill operator. A millwright was an important person in pioneer times, and Joe operated three different mills at three locations. Two mills were sawmills on Rock Creek and Hangman Creek. The last and most famous mill was a grist (flour) mill just below Smythe's Ford and the "Hanging Site," also on Hangman Creek.

Joe Henry was an Americanized version of the man's proper name—Joseph Heinrich. He was a German immigrant and came to this country as a young man. There is no doubt that Joe was well known throughout the region, but strangely almost nothing was ever said about this death and burial.

When I began to get deeply involved with area history, I asked quite a few old-timers what they knew about his last years. This always resulted in only a puzzled look. Finally there was a comment that he was buried in an obscure grave in a quiet rural setting at an old burial site that today is called Rosewood Cemetery. This is three miles south of Fairfield. This was of particular interest to me, most of my immediate family is also buried there. For many years the old-timers called it the "German Cemetery." Considering Joe's German origins this seemed to be a direct fit.

Upon checking old cemetery records, sure enough, he had been buried in an unmarked grave in a far corner of the cemetery. There were no other family members or even any adjoining graves. What was the meaning of this? I had an approximate internment date but there were no death certificate records and there was no obituary information to be found. I checked genealogical and census records—the census figures did list Joe and his family, but nothing else of interest.

For a year and one-half I kept asking old community members, librarians, and archivists about this puzzle. I know a lot of people thought I had too much time on my hands or that I really had a one-track mind—probably the latter is no exaggeration.

Finally an archivist at Eastern Washington University who I told my story to, suggested, "If he owned the mill at the time of his death, the estate had to go through probate. Maybe you could check the county probate records."

In the dim recesses of the county's legal archives I struck pay dirt! Here was a forty-page document—I knew this meant an unusual story would be unfolding. Joe had been committed to the "Insane Asylum" at Medical Lake, as people then called it. Here he spent the last year of his life. The commitment procedure had been a major project. The county sheriff had been involved and that was all part of the probate record. At this time this sort of a happening was a really taboo subject that only family and close friends would even whisper about. This would have been the reason there were no obituaries or newspaper accounts at the time of his death.

(Photo from the Southeast Spokane County Historical Society)

I wrote the story about Joe Henry's life and what I had found in the first article I ever submitted to Nostalgia magazine—a historical monthly in Spokane. Not long after it appeared a lady called me from Sprague, Washington. Joe had been married and had two children—this was part of the old census information. Then later he and his wife divorced. His former wife remarried, the caller was the daughter of Joe's wife with her second husband. This daughter is a half sister to Joe's two sons. These sons are mentioned in various accounts and one of them ran the mill for a year or two after Joe's death.

The caller from Sprague was enthralled to find out what had happened to her mother's first husband. She wanted to visit the grave and the old mill site. She was also able to report that Joe had a surviving son on the east coast.

By this time I had decided that I was going to place a marker on Joe's grave. I decided on the text for a bronze plaque. Then this item had to be made in the eastern U.S. and there were enough delays that it took almost a year to arrive. I mounted it on a small base of concrete and Hangman Creek stone (a nice touch I thought). Finally, I could tell my new friend at Sprague that the grave site was ready for visitors. She and her husband drove over almost immediately. We took pictures at the grave and at the old mill site and had a wonderful visit—sometimes historical research has special bonuses.

A Summary of the Joe Henry Story

(This is an annotated account of the Joe Henry story from the Fairfield Community History of the early 1960's)

In early settlement times there was a big demand for lumber for the settlers to build their homes and barns and for the town people to build stores, schools, churches, etc. Then as the country became built up this demand lessened and the mills became used primarily to grind grain into flour.

In these early times, internal-combustion engines were unknown, so a site where water power could be utilized was of great importance. Quite often they were at a rugged location in a basalt-palisaded canyon where a dam could be built and water run through a mill race with enough fall to provide the mill with power. Frequently this would mean it was at a difficult place to access with horse-drawn wagons to haul in the grain and haul out the flour. This was a common remark about the Joe Henry mill site.

Joe Henry had the skills to build his dam and mill race, erect a big three story mill building, and install the mill stones and other equipment. An understanding of the procedure needed to produce a good quality flow was another final skill. This all took a large amount of industry and talent. Joe's mill was a popular goal for settlers and he had a good business.

However as the story unfolds, Joe had a stubborn and a bull-headed streak. He was said to be "a well-read socialist" and he also had a good deal of sentiment for his German ancestry and original homeland. As World War I came on, these traits developed into the creation of a sizable amount of heat and controversy with fellow community members.

Perhaps even more importantly, the internal-combustion engine was arriving on the scene. Mills were starting to appear in the local towns. People soon began by-passing the long wagon trip back and forth to the Hangman Creek valley.

The traumatic problems of Germany's losses in the war and the decline of mill business probably weighed heavily on Joe. His death occurred in 1917.

This is about where all previous accounts end. The information covered in my introduction leads to a fuller understanding of the story of a man who left his mark in local history. To know the somber parts of his life's ending only add to this saga's pathos and interest.

Another Historic Mill Operation

At a Chapman Lake location local geology created another excellent water power site, capable of supplying excellent water power just below the lake's outlet. This was another example of a site that was comparatively rare and highly prized in pioneer times.

Mill Construction

In the late 1800s several enterprising individuals cooperated to develop a saw mill to provide the first settlers with the lumber needed to build their houses, barns, schools and other buildings needed at that time. The exact date of the initial sawmill construction and operation seems to be in question, however, the grist (flour) mill was constructed in 1897 and operated until 1950. This is the old building still standing on the site. The mill structure is an impressive wood-framed three-story building. It is relatively square, shaped on three sides with a longer sloping add-on at the rear of the building. Today the front of the building still appears straight and plumb, but the exterior wood siding is badly warped and weather-beaten, and the rear wall and its long sloping roof are in complete collapse. Some mill machinery is still at the site but is now twisted and almost indiscernible.

Other surviving features of interest are the mill flume or mill race and the dam that was installed across the lake outlet. The dam significantly increased the lake size and created a higher, more efficient "head" of waterpower to efficiently operate the mill.

Mill Ownership Passes to Pioneer Dybdall Family

Relatively early in the grist mill's operation, a pioneer immigrant by the name of Ole Dybdall bought out the interest of the other owners. He expanded the flour milling operation and acquired a reputation for good service and higher quality flour. He also set up a farming enterprise to help provide for his family.

About 1920 the Dybdall family began a small resort business at the lake to further diversify. This provided an ideal venue for fishing, family outings and other recreational activities that appealed to people of that time. A final feature was added to this selection of enterprises when the family decided a fish hatchery would complement the resort business. This was a very innovative development for these early times.

The entire complex of activities, from the mill's construction through the fish hatchery, showed a resourcefulness and an ability to develop available resources that are the hallmark of pioneer ingenuity and hard work.

Dybdall family members have operated the Chapman Lake activities through several generations. Of course, the days of the mill operation are far in the past. It is said that an application was made a number of years ago and that this mill was accepted for listing on the Historical Preservation Register, however, no restoration work has ever appeared to have been put in place. Evidently the economics and cost have effectively deterred any preservation effort. Today the old mill is a fading derelict of the past, but it can still provide an interesting connection to days long gone by.

A Notable Palouse Pioneer Entrepreneur

Background:

Edward H. Morrison was destined to be a "shaker and a mover" in the realm of farming and business as the Palouse area developed. He was born in August of 1848 in New Jersey. He was a scion of a prosperous family and received a top flight education. After graduating from college he traveled to Europe and studied engineering. The next year he married and he and his wife returned to honeymoon and travel in Europe and the Mediterranean.

When he returned to America he ventured into quite a wide range of business experiences. Then he moved on to some politically related jobs, serving on the 1876 United States Centennial Exposition Commission; then, following that, he was an aid to a congressman in Washington, D.C.

In 1878 he decided to explore options in the western United States and became the registrar of the land office at Walla Walla. From that point he began to become a person of importance in the northern Palouse region.

Little seems to be known about how Morrison acquired the title and began to be known as Colonel Morrison. It is debatable whether he ever had any real military service. One biography does say he was appointed "Commissary General" of the Washington Territory. If that had any connection to this title is a puzzle. We do know that it was not unusual for a person of influence to have this sort of an honorific title.

At this point Morrison had begun extensive dealings in eastern Washington real estate and he aligned himself with large financial interests in the eastern United States. He became their agent and front man. An example of this sort of a connection was a consortium which jointly purchased first 15,000 acres and then 27,000 acres of railroad grant lands. In large areas of the west the railroads were given half of all the land for as much as seventy miles on both sides of newly constructed rail lines. The land that Morrison's cohorts bought was in southern Spokane and northern Whitman counties.

The Marshall Field merchandising empire of Chicago was one of the partners in this group. Their connections to land in this area were to be long lasting as they bought and sold real estate.

Morrison would personally inspect this property and make recommendations on its value, purchase price and terms of sale. This also helped him become a well known individual to the railroads as they built the local lines that opened up the area and created the economic means of marketing the area's crops.

Morrison's Involvements With The North Palouse

Morrison was a man with seemingly unlimited interests. When he picked the Fairfield locale to put down roots, the railroad had just developed a depot and a water tank because of a good watering site for the steam engines. The railroad called this place Regis. Morrison saw the potential and began actively laying out a town site. He wanted a more melodic sounding name and picked Fairfield for his town's name.

He immediately began both business and farming activities on a big scale. By the early 1900's there were over 1,500 acres in the Morrison farm and the Colonel certainly did some interesting farming. Some sixty to one hundred head of horses were used and as many as one hundred to one hundred-fifty men were employed seasonally. Morrison had the connections to acquire leases on so-called "state-land." Sections 16 and 36 of every township were dedicated to the state school system. A section contains 640 acres which was a particularly large contiguous parcel of ground for that period of time. To farm on that scale in the horse-powered days of farming was quite remarkable.

Another of the Colonel's notable farming efforts revolved around his interest

Morrison home with test plots and field hands in the foreground.

in finding specialized crops to grow in the highly fertile and well watered soils of this part of the Palouse. An accompanying picture shows the trial and test plots where a

119

wide assortment of plants was grown.

Vegetable varieties—radish, turnips, onions, cabbage, etc.—were grown and compared. Many species of flowers flourished and bloomed profusely. Grains and legumes were the economic mainstays and they were grown on a large scale. What assured Morrison of lasting fame was his introduction of sugar beets and field peas.

The Dramatic But Short-lived Sugar Boom

With his sugar beet trials Morrison quickly concluded that the soil and weather conditions of this region produced beets with a high sugar content and that this would make them a very attractive endeavor for a big scale crop. He immediately began trying to find financial backing and interest for a prospective new industry. Sugar manufacture was a big national and even an international operation.

Progress at first was slow and disappointing. This was such a new and expensive scheme in the west that a great reluctance was natural, but soon Morrison caught the ear of Daniel C. Corbin. D.C. Corbin was one of the northwest's most prominent tycoons. He had made a huge fortune in railroads, mining and real estate. He had ready access to the big bucks and contacts that it would take to put this project in gear. He liked to do things on a big scale. A sugar beet factory would be a project that big money and big ambitions would push forward with all the resources available.

Washington State Sugar Beet Factory located at Waverly. It was in operation from 1900 to 1910.

The extent of the interest in the proposed sugar beet industry was amazing. All up and down the eastern Palouse promotional meetings were held to stir up the interest of the farmers in this prospective crop.

Now many factors had to come together. A large, centrally located site was needed for the factory. A big supply of water was a necessity, so the little town of Waverly fit the bill and a dam was built and then a rail spur from Fairfield was installed. Waverly quickly grew from a little burg of about two hundred people to a full fledged boom town of a thousand people. The construction of a huge three story brick factory and related facilities cost in the range of $500,000. The cost of construction of homes and businesses is impossible to estimate but it was a staggering investment. The story of this unique plant and its operation along with details about Waverly and its boom town status, and with many rare pictures is the subject of book by this writer—A History of Waverly and Pioneer Life Along This Part of Hangman Creek.

The old rhyme about the "best laid plans of mice and men..." or maybe it was Murphy's Law—decreed the economies of sugar beets were not to be realized in the Palouse. The plant was built and started operating in 1900—it was to run only ten years. Waverly's halcyon days quickly waned and for a long time it nearly slipped into a ghost town status.

The Dry Pea Seed Business

Morrison's enthusiasm for a pea industry in the eastern Palouse was to be much more successful and long lived. Pea production found a ready place in area farming. This crop was used for direct human consumption and the production of seed peas.

Almost every farming town in the eastern Palouse had its own pea seed plant. In those early years big crews of women found fall and winter employment sorting (it was usually called "picking") peas. After a preliminary cleaning operation, peas still needed to roll down a sorting line so that deformed and damaged peas would be "inspected" and removed. In those days of cheap labor there was little thought that eventually these jobs would be completely automated. Now this once important and labor intensive part of local history is almost forgotten. At any rate, Morrison is always credited with being one of the primary founders of our area's pea industry.

Some Morrison Anecdotes

About the turn of the last century, Colonel Morrison had one of the first large combines in the Palouse country. It was a huge, complicated, cumbersome, "ground powered" combine. Ground powered meant it had no engine to operate it but depended on a big traction "bull wheel" to run the combine works. It took over thirty horses to pull a monster machine like this. They were not very successful in the hilly Palouse region. They were difficult to pull at a constant speed and in general had a long list of faults.

This large machine met with a spectacular accident northwest of Fairfield. The "skinner," or horse driver, sat far out in front of the machine and over the horses

121

on a ladder-like extended seat. This gave him a choice view and better control of the horses—he was actually right over the rear horses. This perch would sway and whip as the big machine lurched over rough ground and alternating terrain. The skinner had an important and pivotal job.

Morrison's "ground powered" combine. (Southeast. Spokane County Historical Soc.)

While going down a particularly long and steep hill, the combine began to pick up speed from the effects of gravity and it began to crowd and panic the horses. In this excitement the driver fell or was thrown from his seat. He was crushed as the heavy machine rolled over him. With no one in control the horses began to gallop into a full-fledged runaway and it was impossible for any of the other crew to crawl out on the seat and try to control the horses. Meanwhile, the mechanism of the machine—being ground powered—began to turn at speeds never foreseen by the combine's engineers. The machine literally disintegrated!

One of the few salvageable parts remaining of the combine was its huge thirty-six inch wide "cylinder." This was the component that threshed the seed out of the crops. It was later used on a stationary stand to meticulously thresh crops like radish, turnip, and other small seed vegetables. This was a pretty small compensation for what had once been such a grandiose piece of equipment.

In another unusual mishap, there is an account of Colonel Morrison starting down the road from Fairfield to Waverly. The primitive, high wheeled car he was driving was quite a "mudder," but it was still not up to the challenge of the spring thaw. He drove into a swampy area not far from the present day intersection of Highway 27 and the Waverly Road. The story tells of a crew of about twenty-five men cutting poles and laying planks to build a "corduroy" road to inch the car out of this quagmire. One may well wonder about the good Colonel's comments during this incident!

The Morrison House and Farm

Morrison built a beautiful large home on a hilltop just south of Fairfield that is now the location of the Good Samaritan Retirement Center. The house commanded a terrific view of the town and countryside. It was constructed in quite a lavish colonial style and had a carriage house and other related outbuildings.

The farm headquarters were about a quarter of a mile away just east of town. It was a large complex of barns and a home for the farm manager. In 1932 a spectacular fire destroyed most of these buildings. At that time the family's farming activities were being phased down and the structures were not rebuilt.

Some Unusual Employees and Friends

The meadows below the Morrison house had long been a favored camping place for the local Indians (see photo of Indian encampment on page 19). The Morrisons felt a distinct interest and attachment to these Native Americans. They were allowed to continue to use these sites and the Colonel employed sizable numbers of Indians for seasonal farm work and to help with the labor intensive test plots.

Col. Morrison and Nellie Garry. (Southeast Spokane County Historical Soc.)

Another unusual source of migrant help was Japanese laborers. They were especially important during the sugar beet interval to thin and hoe the beets which were raised as a row crop. One old write-up describes the low area between the big house and the town as "Jap valley," referring to the migrant camp there.

Mrs. Morrison—Louise— was notable for her support of community and church activities. She was a staunch worker for the advancement of the local Presbyterian Church. It was probably here where she became acquainted with Nellie Garry, a widely known Indian person of importance (she is prominently mentioned elsewhere in this book). Nellie was a particular friend to Louise and other women in the family. The local museum has quite a number of pictures showing this connection.

The Morrisons both died in 1914 in the eastern United States. Their two sons continued operating family business interests locally and in Spokane. The Morrison name is firmly entrenched in local history. Again, Morrison laid out the Fairfield town site and owned much property locally. At least one road and many property deeds—notably the upper park in Fairfield—will help continue to recall the Morrison name.

Palouse Pioneer Had A Unique Military Record

Our region's settlement corresponded with a time in history when many of the first pioneers had a record of military service. The Civil War had involved a large part of the nation's men in that long and horrible conflict. Then, for several more decades as the west became increasingly settled, Indian-war campaigns raged over vast areas. Military service was a common experience.

A man who became a prominent pioneer in the Waverly area of the northern Palouse saw military action in such a wide panorama of these conflicts that his story is nothing short of incredible.

William Connolly was born in Ireland in 1840. One of his biographers states that he came to the United States in 1861, "for the purpose of joining the Union Army." At any rate he immediately enlisted in Company F of the Seventeenth U.S. Infantry at Albany, New York With that group he then participated in battles at Harrison's Landing and the Peninsular Campaigns in Virginia's maritime regions. In August of 1862 he was captured, but he was soon paroled and taken to a military hospital in Washington, D.C. From there he was sent to New Jersey and discharged.

Three months later he signed up for another enlistment. Very shortly he was again participating in Virginia battles at Spotsylvania Courthouse, the famous "Wilderness Battle" and then at an engagement at North Ana he was wounded by an artillery shell. His injury was not life threatening and he soon saw more conflict in other regional battles.

Once again Connolly was captured by the southern forces and experienced about nine months in a confederate prison camp. This was in late 1864. He again was paroled and exchanged and after a thirty-day furlough he continued army service until the end of the war.

It might be expected that this much war experience would be enough for anyone, but before long Connolly went to Massachusetts where he joined a unit of the U.S. Cavalry. As this experience unfolded he was destined to be involved in an unbelievable number of campaigns in Indian wars all through the western United States.

His first Indian war experience was fighting against the Utes and the Apaches along the Texas and Mexican borders in 1867. Then in that same general area he fought in actions against the Comanche Indians.

At the end of this enlistment, in 1869, he went out to California. Again, he

124

soon joined up with the cavalry! Before long he was involved in the famous Modoc Indian Wars where renegade Indians holed up in the unusual lava fields in northern California. This locale was extremely rugged and marked with lava flows encompassing deep canyons and fissures that enabled a small contingent of Indians to hold off a large force of soldiers.

"Captain Jack" was the leader of the Indians. He was notorious for his hatred of the whites. He also had the skill and cunning with which he made his small band a major obstacle and force to be reckoned with by the much larger army. Connolly was wounded in one of the attacks on Captain Jack's stronghold, and a little later he was again discharged.

Connolly next drifted up through northeastern Oregon and into the Walla Walla region. He was just in time to be on the scene when the Nez Perce War broke out in 1877. Sure enough, for the last time, Connolly enlisted and took part in this campaign. It was to be his last military action.

Connolly finally seemed to have his fill of wanderlust, and it seemed his yen for action and excitement was fulfilled as well. He soon married and started a family. In 1879 he came to the Waverly area. Here he purchased land and became a prominent farmer and orchardist. Connolly also developed a wide interest in community service. He was involved in organizing the first school and he was active in a variety of fraternal groups. Not surprisingly, the local branch of "The Grand Army of the Republic"—the Civil War veterans' organization—was one of his passions. Another highlight was Connolly's serving on the Spokane County Board of County Commissioners during the years when the courthouse was planned and built in the late 1890's.

Connolly and his wife had six children. The Connolly's are buried in the Waverly Cemetery. William Connolly's unusual exploits are almost forgotten today. A chance reading of some of the old biographies in Edwards' History of Spokane County (1900) by this writer seemed to be an opportunity to recall parts of the dramatic story of a notable pioneer.

Remembrances Of A Waverly Pioneer

Docia Barnes Davies was a sprightly, elderly, white-haired lady by the time this writer knew her. She had a certain flair and style in the way she talked, and her eyes had a sparkle and flash that denoted both humor and a touch of temper. As a girl she had married a middle-aged area farmer who was a widower with children almost her own age. They had children of their own, and Docia knew the hard work of being a mother and a housewife in those early days. They had a large farm, and cooking for crews, raising a large garden and tending to poultry and livestock made for the busiest of lives. In addition, Docia had a gift for being an accurate observer of the community scene.

Docia was born with a serious physical disability. She had a club foot. At that time a surgical remedy for this problem was not readily available, destining her to a life of lameness. The Davies family suffered serious financial reverses and they lost their farm. Docia lived out the last part of her life in conditions not far from poverty. Still she was a respected, well thought of member of the community.

One of the delights of her later years was to be asked to speak about pioneer days at school and community functions. She was also interviewed by various reporters for newspaper articles about the old days in the Waverly area. She brought a special style and a special knowledge of those long ago times that is still of interest to us today.

I have the distinct feeling that Docia would be both pleased and honored to be quoted in this present history. I know I feel privileged to be able to retell the following stories. I have edited and combined three different interviews into the following account.

Waverly in 1897 and After

"When I came to Waverly in 1897 I found an interesting and wonderful town. The families were mostly homesteaders. (Here she names perhaps a dozen and a half families.) They came into town from all around for their mail, hauled by car from Fairfield—the nearest railroad station... There were the people, living in small houses, breaking out these fertile acres from sunflowers, bunch grass, wild roses and service berry bushes; plowing and harrowing by foot, seeding by hand or six-foot drawn by four horses abreast. The horses were small cayuses. It took days from early dawn till dark to put in their crops; wheat was hauled to Spangle, Rosalia and Fairfield for 35 to 65 cents per bushel...

"The sugar beet refinery came; that is a story of its own. And the Spanish-American war took our young men; Clint Lambert was the only soldier wounded; when they came back we gave them a reception to be remembered. We had the best celebrations, visited by governors, politicians; Governor Hay, Senator Dill, Albert Laughon, Del Smith; Judge Webster, speaker of the day, here from Kentucky. We had horse racing, dancing, wrestling, jujitsu, foot racing, rope pulling by young and old...

"World War I took our young men; six never came back. Our service star Legion erected a monument to their honored memories. Governor Hart was here, and a thousand people were here to see and hear for themselves what he said...

Our hometown fairs were wonderful and entertaining to us. Horses, the finest and best: Corey Thayer had his in strings of fours, black Percherons, broad between the eyes, like his stallion trained to stand four feet up on a block, bow his head right and left to his colts and all the people. There was also a Washington state exhibit of riding and driving and draft horses owned by farmers from Latah, Rosalia...

"There were several buggy horses that would take their owners to Spokane in one hour and a few minutes over these early dirt roads...the roads hub deep in dust and mud, the ruts so deep the wagons sometimes stood on two wheels. It took good teamsters to handle the strings on four and six horses with wagons loaded with several tons of dirty beets, and the wheat wagons or racks...

"When the sugar factory boom came our town was prosperous and restless, every home feeding someone else. We had carpenters working all hours, building tabernacles for revival meetings; eleven saloons (editor's note—this does sound exaggerated), three churches, two stables for livery and stage coaching to Fairfield, six stores, four hotels and two of them three-stories high, harness and blacksmith shops, stores of merchandise, Chinese laundry, newspaper, restaurants, two railroads, sidewalks of wood on all the streets... Austin Corbin (D.C. Corbin's son) was here then to see all was progressing his way. No one told him, he told them what to do. All went well. It just had to quit, because the farmers could not grow beets for $6 a ton with handwork and imported labor. Japanese laborers came over in early spring and stayed until harvesting of beets was done. Our men were too long-backed and slow; Japanese were gardeners, quick. They looked like so many toads hopping across those long rows of beets.

"Our post office was then with Charlie Gimble, postmaster, and I, an assistant, handled mail hauled from Fairfield for a thousand people. I was asked to answer letters and address them for Japanese, write the Waverly news items. I knew most every one by his first name and wrote their letters of business and friendship.

"Our history came along by the flow of Hangman Creek Stories and people who never would be if the waters had not stopped long enough to build Waverly and produce food and wealth for hundreds of people of all denominations, creeds and colors; four generations I alone have seen and known, and each pioneer family had a story of its own...

Pioneer Social Affairs in Waverly

"Most of our fun stemmed from our homes and school. The school was the first place for the parents to come for entertainment for their children. School started the first part of September. The weather was generally nice as now in 1960. If someone had a birthday we all gathered outside at noon, ate our lunches in picnic style, played games and sang songs gleefully. We played games such as old cat or any other game that enough youngsters wanted to play. Parents sometimes came and joined in the fun.

"Then there was the County Fair in Spokane. Most of those from here drove up town in hacks or wagons. Some went by train from Fairfield. We all met someplace on the fairgrounds or at the races. We were glad to see each other and talk of the improvements in grain, fruit, chickens, pigs and cattle. I enjoyed the cattle and the clowns, the two-faced wash woman who advertised a new soap, "The Silk Soap," and the clown with a pet pig. Most folks took their lunches. We visited food booths and bought cooking ingredients which we did not have at home.

"One year a lady, Mrs. Know, living between Waverly and Latah, gave birth to four babies on the same day. A.D. Thayer had them shown at the fair for 25 and 50 cent admission in order to help these parents get a few dollars for the winter. Although I had seen them dozens of times, I had to take another look and buy a picture; I have it yet. After riding on a musical merry-go-round we came home from the fair

full of new ideas, and they were generally happy ones."
This concludes the Docia Davis remembrances of Waverly pioneers. The following adds more details to the story of "the Quadruplets of the Palouse."

The following account was recorded in the Fairfield Community History by one of the family's neighbors.

The Know family lived in primitive and cramped pioneer quarters on an isolated farm. One night in June 1897, Mr. Know came to get our mother and another lady on the next farm to help Dr. Ensley receive the four new babies, three girls and a boy, which were proving too much for him. They were named Leona, Leola, Leota and Leon. The news of their birth spread rapidly, and people came from far and near to see them. The babies were shown at the Spokane Fair in the fall. This was arranged by concerned neighbors. The family was in dire financial straits.

Later in the fall while Mr. Know and a bachelor neighbor were away to get winter fuel, Mrs. Know was seated at her sewing machine, with the two older children playing beside her and her four babies asleep on the bed in the room. She saw a spark fall on her work and looked up to see the whole ceiling ablaze. She snatched up the four infants, quilts and all, pushed the children ahead of her and dashed outside. She laid the babies on the snow-covered ground, gave the two and four year-old children sticks to keep a hog away from the precious bundle, then rushed back and dragged out a trunk that held her mother's picture. Just as she got out the door the whole roof fell in behind her.

Gathering up her infant burden, wrapped warmly in the quilts, she bade Virgie and Jim to follow her and trudged bravely through the falling snow a quarter of a mile to the home of the bachelor neighbor. Laying her tiny baby bundle on the porch, she took the axe to chop open the locked door, went in and built a fire in the wood stove to keep her small charges from the increasing cold. There, the absent men found her that night, homeless but undaunted. Sometime later the infants became ill, and two died. The two surviving children grew into adulthood.

Smith and Beall

A pair of early regional pioneers had ties to Palouse region history in an interesting way. John Smith and Thomas Beall appeared on the scene very early in connection with the local Indian hostilities in 1858. They fit into the rare category of being civilians hired as packers for the U.S. Army when the military mounted major travel maneuvers or campaigns.

John Smith served in the September 1858 Colonel George Wright campaign against this area's Indians. After he ended his Army-related service, he continued to work a while as a packer, transporting supplies to various mining venues. Eventually he married and began ranching and farming. He ended up settling northwest of Deep Creek near the Lincoln County line. He is buried in a pioneer cemetery about five miles north of Deep Creek. Some of his descendants still live in the Worley, Idaho area.

Tom Beall had several special claims to fame. We first hear of him as a head civilian packer for the Steptoe Campaign. Surviving that event you might think he would have been leery of the military, however, four months later he was back on board again with the Wright campaign.

Beall had a knack for attaining a degree of notoriety. In the Steptoe affair he is sometimes placed in the position of being at fault for the notorious problem of the lack of ammunition that was to be a key factor in the expedition's defeat. Some reports even say he discarded ammunition in favor of whiskey! Beall vehemently denied this allegation, and it was certainly never more than a rumor. Serving with the Wright forces, Beall again comes to the fore in an infamous way when he was designated to be the hangman for the Indian captives who were to be meted out an immediate death sentence.

Reportedly Beall was the only man admitting to be adept at tying a "hangman's noose." It also became part of the story that he received $20.00 for each hanging—and again Beall later denied he was paid a bonus for this grizzly task.

Like Smith, Beall became involved in packing and freighting. Still later he became involved with Lewiston and Snake River area transportation and stagecoaching.

Beall again appeared on the local scene when a major effort was begun to memorialize the Steptoe Battle site in the early 1900s. He and several other survivors first helped verify the location. After the long process it took to acquire the site and raise funds for the monument, the survivors were special guests at the dedication in June of 1914.

A Final Pilgrimage

A big event for both Smith and Beall was a return pilgrimage to revisit the old historic sites of the 1858 Wright campaign. The two old white-haired and white-bearded gentlemen made a memorable sight as they returned to the old locations at Four Lakes, Spokane Plains and the "Horse Slaughter Camp" site. (This location is within sight of the place known as Spokane Bridge.) Perhaps the most notable stop of all was the "Hanging Camp" site on Hangman Creek. This location in the heart of the north Palouse drew them like a magnet to the campaign's ending rendezvous with destiny. These places and events were to insure them a prominent place in regional history.

Tom Beall and John Smith, survivors of the Indian War of 1858, revisit the infamous hanging site in about 1910. By this time, the busy byway had lost most of its traffic of soldiers, traders, miners, and settlers.

Scene at the dedication of the Steptoe battlefield monument. (Photo from the Northwest History Room, Spokane City Library)

130

EPILOGUE

A Final Introspection

This look at Northern Palouse history began with an emphasis on the boundaries and borders of the region and how they connect to the local streams, especially Hangman Creek and partly to smaller, neighboring Pine Creek. This is a region that stretches across parts of two counties in eastern Washington and two counties in northwestern Idaho. It encompasses an area of nearly 500,000 acres of land and is bigger than Rhode Island.

Quite a few of the stories we have looked at have focused on history that connects to these landmark streams. Name controversies, treaty camps, mill sites, trail and road crossings all seem to be interrelated.

The Name Controversy

We have seen that one of the most colorful aspects of local history in the northern Palouse is the name controversy that centers around its primary stream.

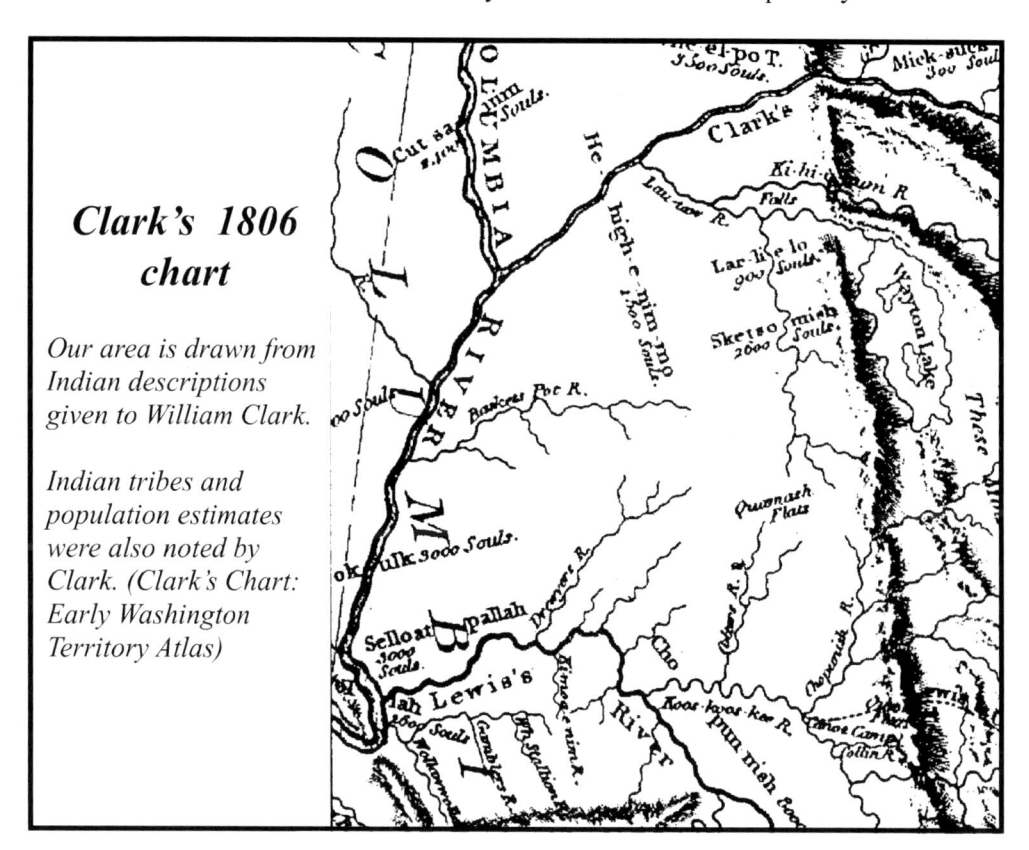

Clark's 1806 chart

Our area is drawn from Indian descriptions given to William Clark.

Indian tribes and population estimates were also noted by Clark. (Clark's Chart: Early Washington Territory Atlas)

This graphic is copied from an 18x24 inch colored poster which is a project of the Spokane County Conservation District. The poster text has a good summary of historical facts and details. The poster may still be available at the district's office.

When Lewis and Clark came through the Inland Northwest, charting and mapping the new territories was their main priority. They did not travel very far north of the Snake River region. They did make a distinct effort to get descriptions of this region from the Indians along their route. As a result, they learned something about our local river systems. They thought the Spokane region's rivers ran much farther to the northwest before draining into the Columbia River, and on their charts this whole river system was called the Lau-taw.

A number of interpretations of that name later evolved to the southeastern tributary of the Spokane River, and it began to be called the Lah-too, which further evolved into Latah Creek. We should note at this point that Latah also became the name for Latah County in Idaho. That connection is always agreed to be a Nez Perce Indian name, and this tribe is of a very different language family than our local Spokane and Coeur d'Alene Indians.

About the only name that has come down in history from local tribes (the Salish) is the "Sin-too-too-ooley," and it has been used only rarely. Lau-taw or Lah-too does not seem to appear anywhere in the Salish languages.

The name situation got even more confused when local explorations began in the mid-1800s. The military forces were one of the primary mappers during this period. On Army maps appear the names "Camas Prairie Creek" and "Nedl-Whauld." Camas Prairie Creek is a natural, because much of the upper watershed is a major Camas harvesting area. But the Nedl-Whauld name only adds more confusion. Is it an Indian name? If so, it has no known definition. Some historians speculate that there may have been a fur trapper in the stream basin called Ned Whauld. Feel free to make your own call on this matter!

It was in 1858 that the real crux of the name debate came to the fore. Col. George Wright came into the region with a well-armed force to settle the Indian unrest. In a number of battles he effectively subdued the Indians and extracted stringent treaty terms and meted out punishments. His last treaty that came in this campaign was on this stream about twenty miles from Spokane. An important part of the proceedings at this location was the hanging of seven Indian warriors. This was the event that initiated the Hangman Creek name in our area history. Much of the following mapping in the region quickly adopted that name.

Today, most of the residents in the watershed use the Hangman Creek name, but there have long been objections that it is too gruesome and bloody a term. Today you might hear, "It is not politically correct." Spokane County and the State of Washington both passed legislation to make Latah Creek the official name. However, all Federal agencies retain the Hangman Creek usage on their maps.

Farther upstream the creek crosses the Idaho state line, and the headwaters rise on the Coeur d'Alene Indian Reservation. On all of its maps, Idaho uses the Hangman Creek name, and the major tributary of the stream is called "Little Hangman Creek." Finally, the Coeur d'Alene Tribe uses the Hangman Creek name on their tribal records. Tribal Council members say the historical significance of the name's origin makes it an appropriate designation.

Just a few years ago a national organization called the United States Board on Geographic names held their national convention in Spokane. Most of its members are college staff people or governmental agency members. High on the convention agenda was a close look at our local streams name controversy. The convention group took a bus tour, with the Colonel Wright treaty camp site as their first stop. This writer spoke to the group about the local history aspects of this spot and said that as a resident of the watershed he unequivocally supported the Hangman Creek usage. Later in the convention proceedings the group passed an advisory vote of approval for the Hangman Creek name.

Over a long period of time this stream has had a long and unusual list of names. As we look at the current status, we may admit that the decision of local lawmakers regarding the Latah Creek usage was perhaps well-intended; however, the people closest to the scene, who speak about the stream on a daily basis, continue to use the colorful and historic name of Hangman Creek.

Back to Elizabeth Marion

Concluding these accounts of northern Palouse history, some of the prose of Elizabeth Marion helps provide the final bookend of this look at the area's past. She observed: "Times change, many things are gone, with a little murmur of anecdote and nostalgia in their wake." The native prairie chicken of eighty-some years ago is gone. The deer, beaver and coyotes have withstood every assault. Roads once in frequent use have returned to field and brush. One-room schoolhouses in neighborhood vantage spots are gone, and only their names linger in the local vocabulary.

"Most of all, the creek has changed. Only in its first few miles is it still the pristine stream of long ago. Road builders, railroad crews, conservation engineers and farmers all have shoved the creek around, changing it here and there with channeling and diking. Once dammed to wash sugar beets and run grist and saw mills, it is still used by farmers and stockmen. And who can forget the Japanese gardeners, whose green geometry and green thumbs decorated its last miles through the approaches to Spokane.

"From its watershed slopes on a green Idaho divide to its mouth inside a mushrooming city, Hangman's is not a long journey." It is an historic one! In a land where legends are few and modern man is mainly too busy to make much of them, some stories do linger from the past. I do hope they give some inspiration and understanding!"

Inspiration and understanding? This editor certainly hopes so—these stories about the history of the Palouse say something important about what it took to build this place and what it was like along the way. They are lessons and examples that we should not easily forget.

BIBLIOGRAPHY

SOURCES:

Durham, Nelson W.   History of the City of Spokane, State of Washington, Vol. II
S. J. Clark Publishing Co., 1912

Edwards, Rev. Jonathan   Illustrated History of Spokane, Washington, County, State of Washington
W. H. Lever, Publisher, 1900

Coleman, Lewis and
Rieman, Leo   The Mullan Road
B. C. Payette, Publisher, 1980

Fahey, John   Jay P Graves, University of Washington Press, 1987

Saving The Reservation
University of Washington Press, 2004

Fuller, Emmaline   Left By the Indians
Ye Galleon Press, 1980

History of North Idaho: Northern Counties, State of Idaho
Western Historical Publishing Co., 1903

Illustrated History of Whitman County, State of Washington
W. H. Lever Publisher, 1901

Kingston, Celyon   The Inland Empire in the Pacific North West
Ye Galleon Press, 1981

Kowrack, Edward J   Saga of the Coeur d'Alene Indians
Ye Galleon Press, 1991

Leitz, Glenn   Spring Valley - Its History
Self-published, 1998

A History of Waverly
Self-published, 1999

Lewis, William S.   "Statement" of Nellie Garry
Manuscript, 1916, Joel E. Ferris Library/Archives,
Museum of Arts and Culture

Mullan, Lt. John   Miners and Travelers Guide
Ye Galleon Press, 1991

Report of the Construction of a Military Road from
Fort Walla Walla to Fort Benton
Ye Galleon Press, 1998

Nelson, Amanda Wimpy   My Sister and I

Ye Galleon Press, 1973

Peltier, Jerome   Felix Warren - Pioneer Stage Driver
Ye Galleon Press, 1988

Manring, Benjamin Franklin
Conquest of the Coeur d'Alenes, Spokanes and Palouse
Ye Galleon Press, 1975

Stevens, Herbert   Vigilantes Ride in 1882
Ye Galleon Press, 1988

Weber, Bert   Postmarked Washington, Vol. I
Ye Galleon Press, 1987

Widman, E. J.   Browsing the Rosalia Citizen, 1904-1909
Self Published

OTHER SOURCES:

COMMUNITY HISTORIES:

Early History of Fairfield. Town and Country Study, 1960

Mount Hope Community Study - 1887-1938, 1980

Rosalia. Battle Ground to Wheat Fields, 1858-1988, Community Committee 1988

The Tekoa Story, From Bunch Grass to Grain, 1962
Community Development, History Committee

On the Battle Ground. Rosalia Chamber of Commerce, 1909

Fairfield, Washington. Fairfield Commercial Club
(Oregon-Washington R.R. & Navigation Co. and Sunset Magazine cooperating) 1910

ATLASES, NEWSPAPERS, MAGAZINES AND OTHER PUBLICATIONS:

Agricultural Bureau - 100th Anniversary - 1897-1997.
Spokane Chamber of Commerce, 1997

Chas. Ogle Atlas of Spokane County, 1912

Historical Maps of Idaho Territory.
Western Washington Publications, 1972

Historical Maps of Washington Territory
Western Washington Publications, 1972

North Palouse Journal
33 W. Emma St., Rockford, Washington 99030

136

Palouse Magazine
P.O. Box 324, Garfield, Washington 99130

Nostalgia Magazine
1703 N. Normandie, Spokane, Washington 99205

The U.S. Department of Interior/Geological Survey
The Channeled Scablands of Eastern Washington, 1981

The Bunch Grass Historian
Whitman County Historical Society

The Pacific Northwesterner
Spokane Corral of the Westerners

The Gold Historians
Coulee Dam, Washington. 99133
(Published in the 1980s. Now discontinued. Can be found in some library reference departments)

Whitman County Atlas, 1910

ACKNOWLEDGEMENTS:

Northwest History Room, Spokane City Library

Northwest Museum of Arts and Culture
Joel E. Ferris Library/Archives

Files of the Southeast Spokane County Historical Society
Selected Stories

INDEX

A
Adams, Glen..................................1, 31, 41
Almota...57
Alpha..81
Anderson Family.............................31, 35
Aquatic Animals..................................95

B
Badger...94
Beale, Thomas...........................128-129
Buffalo..91
Bitterroot Mountains............................10
Bretz, J. Harland..................................8

C
Camas Prairie Creek...........................133
Cemeteries
    Butte..87
    Lone Pine.....................................86
    Mount Hope..................................84
    Riggs...88
    Rosewood...................................114
    Sanders Creek..............................87
Calhoun, Andrew J...............................31
Chapman Lake...................................61
Churches
    Bethel Methodist............................39
    Mount Hope..................................84
    Lone Pine.....................................87
    Spring Valley.................................89
Clark, Lucy (Mrs. I. H.)....................85, 86
Clark, Capt. William...........................131
Colfax...57
Connolly, Fr. Thomas E., S.J..................20
Connolly, William........................124, 125
Coeur d'Alene Lake...............................9
Coeur d'Alene Indians..........................15
    Mission and School........................16
    Economics, Politics and
    the Reservation............................16
Coplen family....................................112
Coyote..94
Curlew..81
Curlew Bird..92

D
Davies, Docia..............................125-128
Davis, J. S. (Cashup)............................57
Davis, Mary Ann.............................58-59
Darknell..82
Darknell, Clara...................................82
Darknell, Grace..................................34
Desmet - Joset (Missionaries)................4
Duncan...81
Dybdall Family.................................117

E
Eid, Norma..40

F
Eastern Washington Historical Society....112

F
Fairbanks..83
Fairfield....................................73, 119
Farmington..10
Favorite, J. J......................................49
Fuller, Emmaline................................27

G
Garry, Joseph.....................................20
Garry, Ignace.....................................20
Garry, Nellie........................19, 21, 124
Garry, Spokane..................................18
Glacial Flooding...................................6
Graves, Jay P.....................................70
Grist Mills.......................................114

H
Harris, Ed...42
Hart, William.....................................96
Hangman Creek
    Differing Names...........................134
    Watershed.............................10, 132
Heinrichs, Joseph (Joe Henry)..............114
Hole-in-the-Ground...............................8
Homesteading....................................46
"Horse Slaughter Camp"....................129

I
Indians
    Coeur d'Alene..........................13, 15
    Palouse..................................13, 15
    Spokane.......................................13
Indian Panics...................26, 32, 58

J
Jackrabbits.......................................93

K
Kentuck Trail..................................2, 64
Know Quadruplets.............................127

L
Lapwai Trail..................................59-60
Lah-too or Lau-taw............................113
Lava Flows..6
Latah..10, 80
Latah Earthquake Fault........................19
Lederer, Alice....................................34
Lewis and Clark................................133
Lockwood..82
Lone Pine..85
Loess...6
Lovell Valley......................................21

M
Mammoths......................................135

138

Manifest Destiny..14
Maps
    Current reference..45
    Glacial floods..8
    Land Survey - 1873.....................................46
    Railroads..67, 71
    Regional Map - 1860s....................................5
    Regional Map - 1870....................................6
    Spokane-Whitman County..........................54
    Rosalia Post Office......................................49
    Waverly Township......................................53
Masterson, Billy...41
Marion, Elizabeth.................................1, 2, 136
Mining..77
Mooney, Cornelius..36
Morris, Tum..32
Morrison, Col. Edward.....................................118
Mount Hope..84
Mullan, Lt. John..2, 60
Mullan Road...64

N
Neil, Aldy..38
Nelson, Amanda Wimpy....................................24
Newspapers
    Citizen - Rosalia..97
    Sentinel - Tekoa..105
    Standard - Fairfield....................................97
    Times - Spokane Falls................................72
North Palouse Journal...98
Nostalgia Magazine..115

O
Oil Exploration...78

P
Palouse
    Boundaries..9
    Name...14
    River..15
Palouse Magazine...1
Palus...14
Pea Seed Industry...121
Pine City..8
Pine Creek..11
Pine Grove..58, 82
Pioneer Picnics
    Dau's Grove..108
    Fry's Grove...109
    German Insurance Picnic.........................107
    Old Settlers Picnics..................................109
    Smyth's Ford Picnic.................................111
Prairie Chicken...92
Prairie View School..88

Q
Qualchan..2

R
Railroads
    North Coast...70

O.W.R.&N..66
    Spokane-Inland Empire Electric................66
Railroad Maps..67, 71
Rattlers Run...33, 63
Roads and maps...60
Rock Creek...11
Rock Creek Post Office......................................51
Rock Creek Trestle...68
Rosalia..30, 50
Rosalia Chamber of Commerce.........................73
Rustlers and Vigilantes......................................38

S
Seltice, Andrew..17
Setters...82
Smith, John...128
Snake River..8, 57
Spangle...58
Song Birds..93
Spokane County Conservation District............132
Spokane Falls...72
Steptoe Butte..7
Steptoe Campaign...129
Steptoe Monument..129
Spring Valley..69, 83
Spring Valley Church...83
Spring Valley Depot...69
Squirrels...94
Stagecoaches..65
Stevens, Herb..1, 39
Stevens County..52
Sugar Beets..120
Smythe's Ford.........................4, 11, 40, 127
Smythe's Ford Monument.......................111, 127

T
Technology changes...55
Tekoa..105
Territorial Road..59
Texas Ferry Road...59
Townships..46, 52

U
United States Board on
Geographic Places..134

V
Vole (mouse)..94

W
Warren, Felix..36, 65
Waverly..3, 121
    Boom Town Status...................................121
    Waverly Butte Mining................................79
Whitman, John M...30
Williams, Anasta..22
Wimpy Family..24, 36
Wright, Col. George...3
Wright Campaign...128

139